*The Life and Teaching of*
# THE
# PROPHET MUHAMMAD

*The Life and Teaching of*
# THE
# PROPHET MUHAMMAD

*Mohd. Abdul Rauf,* J.M.N.,
Alimiyah (Azhar), M.A. (Cantab),
Ph.D. (London)

ISLAMIC PUBLICATIONS BUREAU,
LAGOS, NIGERIA.

© Copyright M. A. Rauf, 1996

U.S.A.
**AL-SAADAWI PUBLICATIONS**
P.O. Box 4059
Alexandria, VA 22303
Tel: (703) 329-6333
Fax: (703) 329-8052

LEBANON
**AL-SAADAWI PUBLICATIONS**
P.O. Box 135788
Sakiat Al-Janzir
Vienna Bldg., Vienna St.
Beirut, Lebanon
Tel: 860189, 807779

All rights reserved. No part of this publication may be reproduced, stored in retrieval system, or transmitted in any form or by any means, electronic, mechanical, photo-copying, reproducing or otherwise, without the prior permission of the publisher.

*THE LIFE AND TEACHINGS OF*
*THE PROPHET MUHAMMAD*

First Edition, 1416 AH/1996 CE

Cover design by Object Design and Comm., Inc.

ISBN # 1-881963-58-6 PB

Printed in the USA

# Foreword

During the course of 1960, several authorities on Islam were invited to give broadcast talks over Radio Malaya with a view to explaining Islam to the non-Muslims in the country. Dr M.A. Rauf, the Principal of the Muslim College, Malaya, was one of the authorities who were invited to give such talks. His talks were very much appreciated by those who followed them. This book contains the texts of his talks. The purpose of this book therefore is to enable those who did not have the opportunity of listening to these stimulating talks to read them in print.

Although the official religion of the Federation of Malaya is Islam, more than 50 per cent of the inhabitants of the country are non-Muslims, and in view of this it is desirable that the non-Muslims be informed of the principles of Islam and the teaching of the Prophet Muhammad to enable them to understand and appreciate the religion.

In his talks Dr Rauf touched on subjects which have frequently been misunderstood by some non-Muslims and even by some of those Muslims who have had Western education. Dr Rauf clearly and simply explained the teaching of the Prophet Muhammad on such subjects as tolerance in Islam, polygamy and that Islam thrives by its teaching and not by the sword, as some people may have been led to believe. Indeed, Islam has been a stabilizing factor in this world of instability especially at the present time when materialism counts more than anything else.

Dr Rauf has done a splendid work by publishing his talks, and I am sure they will be welcomed by those who wish to know more about Islam and even by those who already know about Islam.

*Syed Ja'afar Albar*
FORMERLY ASSISTANT MINISTER OF
INFORMATION AND BROADCASTING

# Contents

|  |  | page |
|---|---|---|
| Foreword by Syed Ja'afar Albar | | v |
| Preface | | viii |

*Chapters*

| | | |
|---|---|---|
| ONE | The Arabian Background | 1 |
| TWO | Mecca and the Ka'bah | 9 |
| THREE | Muhammad's Birth and Upbringing | 19 |
| FOUR | The Mission and Early Converts | 26 |
| FIVE | Reaction of Mecca to the Mission | 33 |
| SIX | Persecution and Endurance | 38 |
| SEVEN | Yathrib (Madinah), and Glimpses of Success | 45 |
| EIGHT | The Hijrah | 51 |
| NINE | Reforms and Consolidation | 57 |
| TEN | Hostile Relations with Mecca | 65 |
| ELEVEN | Major Military Engagements | 71 |
| TWELVE | Further Hostilities, and the Truce of Hudaibiyah | 78 |
| THIRTEEN | Marriages of the Prophet | 85 |
| FOURTEEN | Conquest of Mecca | 93 |
| FIFTEEN | The Last Two Years | 100 |
| | Bibliography | 107 |
| | Glossary of Arabic Terms | 108 |
| | Index | 109 |

# Preface

The following pages consist of a series of lectures delivered by the author over Radio Malaya during the years 1958 and 1959, when he was serving as the Principal of the Muslim College Malaya, the first institution of higher Islamic education ever established in Malaya (now Malaysia). When the Kuala Lumpur Representative of Longmans, a leading publishing house in London, England, wrote to his Headquarters in London about the popularity of those lectures, especially among the non-Muslim communities in the country who constituted about half of the population, as reflected in the local newspapers which reported that many members of those communities wrote to Radio Malaya requesting copies of the lectures, Longmans decided to have those lectures published in the form of a book. The project was completed in 1964.

As the author was recently urged to have these lectures re-published, Brother Safaa Al-Saadawi graciously agreed to fulfill this task and undertook to have the reproduced copy distributed.

There is nothing so inspiring, so sweet, or so delightful as reading the beautiful story of the most accomplished, the most perfect, and yet the modest man, Muhammad Ibn Abd Allah, the Last Messenger of Almighty Allah, peace and blessings be upon him. From the beginning of his life, Almighty God protected him from all the pitfalls of the Jahiliyyah age. Even when his family pressed him to join them in a session of their idol worship when he was still a boy, the Angels, assuming human shape and dressed in white, intervened, standing between him and the idols. It is related that his uncle Abu Talib became offended when his repeated urgings to young Muhammad to join them in their idol worship were not heeded, so much so that members of his clan feared that their idols might hurt them. So they told him: "O Muhammad! We are afraid of the consequences of your avoidance of our gods. You never join in our festival (religious) celebrations." They pressed him so hard that we went once to join in these celebrations, but he suddenly returned quite frightened. They asked him: "What happened?" He said: "I am afraid that I have been a victim of a Satanic touch." The retorted: "No. God the Almighty would not let you suffer a Satanic touch in view of your perfect virtues. Let us know what happened (when you went to the idols)." Muhammad said: "Whenever I attempted to get close to the idol (called Bawanah), I saw (in between) a tall white figure, an Angel, shouting: "Go away, O Muhammad. Do not touch it." Umm Ayman who related the story and who was one of Muhammad's wet nurses, added: "Muhammad, since then, never participated in a Qurashite festival until he began to receive the Divine Revelations (from Heaven)."

Al-Halabi, a renowned biographer of the Prophet states:

"Allah protected Muhammad, peace and blessings be upon him, since his tender, from all the filthy Jahiliyyah practices and from all their blemishes. (Allah made him) in the shape and manner that were in keeping with his noble Prophetic character, so much so that he was the best mannered person, the most truthful, the most honest, and the farthest among them from abominations, and became recognized as the most meritorious, and the best among his people."

(Al-Sirah Al-Halabiyyah, 1384/1964, vol. I, p. 199).

# Maps and Illustrations

|   |   | page |
|---|---|---|
| 1. | Opening chapter of the Qur'an (India Office Library) | xii |
| 2. | Arabia and its neighbours at the time of the Prophet Muhammad | 3 |
| 3. | A southern Arabian inscription (British Museum) | 4 |
| 4. | Petra (Paul Popper) | 5 |
| 5. | A camel | 6 |
| 6. | Bedouines | 7 |
| 7. | A caravan | 8 |
| 8. | A general view of Mecca (Paul Popper) | 9 |
| 9. | Zamzam (Paul Popper) | 10 |
| 10. | The Ka'bah (Paul Popper) | 11 |
| 11. | Lineal descent of the Prophet Muhammad | 16 |
| 12. | Earliest part of Qur'anic Revelation (first 5 verses of Chapter 96, appearing in the three lines on the top) (India Office Library) | 27 |
| 13. | The Mosque at Quba' (From "Mecca the Blessed, Madinah the Radiant" by Emil Esin, published by Elek Books Ltd.) | 52 |
| 14. | Pilgrims | 59 |
| 15. | Letter supposed to have been sent by the Prophet to al-Mundhir (as published in ZDMG) | 83 |
| 16. | The Mosque of Madinah (From "Mecca the Blessed, Madinah the Radiant" by Emil Esin, published by Elek Books Ltd.) | 104 |

## (١) سُورَةُ الفَاتِحَةِ
### مَكِّيَّةٌ وَآيَاتُهَا سَبْعٌ

بِسْمِ اللَّهِ الرَّحْمَنِ الرَّحِيمِ ۝ الْحَمْدُ لِلَّهِ رَبِّ الْعَالَمِينَ ۝ الرَّحْمَنِ الرَّحِيمِ ۝ مَالِكِ يَوْمِ الدِّينِ ۝ إِيَّاكَ نَعْبُدُ وَإِيَّاكَ نَسْتَعِينُ ۝ اهْدِنَا الصِّرَاطَ الْمُسْتَقِيمَ ۝ صِرَاطَ الَّذِينَ أَنْعَمْتَ عَلَيْهِمْ غَيْرِ الْمَغْضُوبِ عَلَيْهِمْ وَلَا الضَّالِّينَ ۝

نَزَلَتْ بَعْدَ المُدَّثِّرِ

*Opening chapter of the Qur'an*

# ONE

# The Arabian Background

In a study of the biography of the Prophet Muhammad and his teaching, it is proper to begin by a discussion of the Arabian background. This in fact is the theme of this initial talk; but before embarking on the subject a few preliminary remarks have to be made.

In the first place I wish to discuss the way in which the word *Muhammad* is to be pronounced. Muhammad is a name, an Arabic name; and I have spelled it in the way the Arabs pronounce it. The familiar European version, 'Mohammed', has the vowels o and e in place of u and a. H. W. Fowler in his book, *Dictionary of Modern English Usage*,[1] advocates a third version, 'Mahomet', which appears to be the oldest English form. Fowler says, '*Muhammad* (with a dot under the h to indicate the peculiar Arabic sound) should be left to the pedants, *Mohammed* to historians and the like, while ordinary mortals should go on saying and writing in newspapers and novels and poems and such reader's matter, what their fathers said before them.'[2] For the sake of uniformity and in view of the closer contacts now prevailing, what Fowler considers to be pedantic should, I think, become the common form of pronouncing *Muhammad*.

In the second place, it is important that we should not be misled by the title of this series of talks, *The Life and Teaching of the Prophet Muhammad*. We should not be led to understand that Muhammad was the author of the teaching he delivered to his followers. It is all believed to have been the revelation from God, the Almighty; and Muhammad was merely chosen to be the instrument through which the Islamic teaching was passed on to the creatures of God.

The third point I want to make clear at this early stage is that the teaching brought about by the Prophet Muhammad does not need to be fundamentally different from that taught by earlier prophets, such as Abraham, Moses and Christ.

The fundamental part of a religion, as far as we can see, is the ideas about God and His relation to the world, and the ideas about those whom God selected to be His Messengers. This part deals with truths; and truths cannot change with the passage of time. Muslims believe therefore, that their faith is identical with the original faiths taught in earlier religions before they were tampered with through misunderstanding and through other factors. In addition to this similarity of faith, other striking similarities can be easily found in the ethical teachings of those religions. In this connection a Qur'anic verse reads:

*"He had instituted for you in religion What He has laid up on Noah, and that which We have revealed unto you and that which We had instituted for Abraham, Moses and Jesus, commanding: Establish your religion and do not divide into parties regarding it."*

The Prophet Muhammad was born in Arabia round the year 570 of the Christian era, and died in the year 632. There he spent all his life and he was never out of the peninsula except when he made two commercial trips to Syria in the early part of his life. However, a biography of the Prophet cannot be written without some consideration of the background of the environment in which he was born and in which he lived and to whose inhabitants he first delivered his message. We shall therefore say a few words about Arabia and its early inhabitants.

Some authorities[4] claim that Arabia was originally a fertile country, with rivers, canals and dams. Through the millenia,

THE ARABIAN BACKGROUND 3

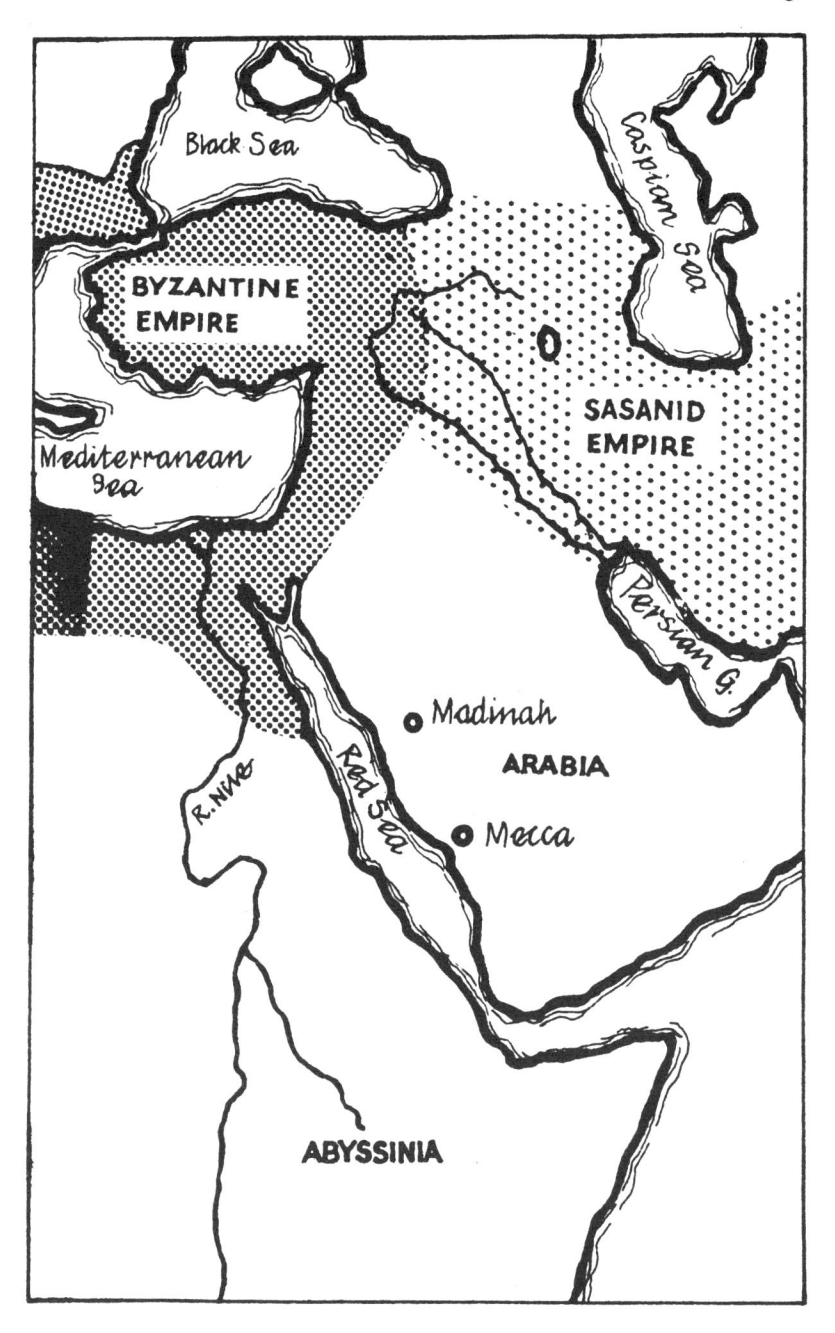

*Arabia and its neighbours at the time of the Prophet Muhammad*

they assert, water receded towards the north, the land gradually dried up, and the desert grew at the expense of fertile land. As a result of this process, the country was over-populated, and waves of emigration into the Fertile Crescent took place.

Historical Arabia, however, consists of seas of sandy deserts and ranges of rocky mountains with severe climatic conditions. The only exception is the south-western corner where the Yemen lies. In the desert rain may fall here and there during the season of winter giving rise to the growth of patches of grass from which livestock can be fed. In the oases, where water gathers in wells, orchards of date palms and some cereals are grown.

The southern Arabians established glorious kingdoms, most renowned among these was the Kingdom of *Saba'*. They were the builders of the first sky-scrapers in history. Their

*A southern Arabian inscription*

*Petra*

inscriptions and other findings some of which have been recently discovered, show the high degree of civilization they had attained. Some of these southern tribes emigrated to the north and established kingdoms in Palmyra and Petra which developed important relations with Rome. These kingdoms declined before the advent of Islam, and the Yemen itself fell under the yoke of Abyssinia. It became later a Persian colony and it continued as such until it was delivered by Islam. However, two Arab tribes, the Chassanids and the Lakkmids established two buffer kingdoms which remained till the advent of Islam. The first was in Syria as a satellite of Byzantium, and the other was established in Iraq as a satellite of Persia.

The inhabitants of central and northern Arabia, on the other hand, were on the whole nomadic, shifting from one place to another in search for water and pasture. The camel was the best asset in the desert, because of its stamina, forebearance and the peculiar shape of its feet. In addition to its use as a beast of burden, the camel, together with sheep and goats gave the Bedouin milk to drink, meat to eat, fur and wool to weave his clothes and skins to build his house of tents. The Qur'an reminds the Arabs of these favours in the following words:

*A camel*

"*Allah has made of your houses rest and comfort for you; and has provided for you, from the skin of the cattle, houses which are light for you on the day you travel and on the day you stay; and from their wool, and their fur and their hair, comfort and enjoyment for an appointed term.*"[5]

The hard life of the Bedouin was reflected in his manners. He was ill-tempered, unruly and aggressive; but the Arabs since early times cultivated certain virtues which they held in great esteem and of which they sang in their poetry. Courage, manliness, generosity and self-respect were eminent among these virtues.

The difference in climatic conditions and cultural attainment between the south and the north was reflected in the relationship between the Southern and Northern Arabs. Although they claimed a common ancestry, they had developed since early times a mutual mistrust and mutual tension. The Southerners looked upon the northern people as primitive and lacking in civilization, while the Northerners looked upon the Southerners as a soft, sedate and less-adventous type of people. This tension survived the advent of Islam and, to no small extent, influenced the turn of events in the early Islamic centuries.[6]

The pre-Islamic Arabs lived in consanguineous groups which they called tribes, united internally by their blood ties. Each group believed themselves to have descended from one ancestor in the male line. The social unit was the tribe or clan. The individual identified his interests with those of the rest of the tribe. An offence against a member of the tribe was an offence against the tribe as a whole, to be revenged by all its members. The chief of a tribe held an eminent position, and its elders formed a council or *majlis*.

An important economic feature of the pre-Islamic Arabia were the trade routes running from the South to the North, and in other directions. The caravans marched through these routes carrying the products of India, the silk of China, the

*Bedouins*

*A caravan*

gold dust from Africa and the products of the Middle East.

On the caravan routes certain commercial centres developed, prominent among which was Mecca. It was in this town that the Prophet was born.

[1] Oxford University Press, 1957, pp. 338–9.
[2] P. 339.
[3] Chapter XLII, v. 13.
[4] I.e., Winkler and Caetani, quoted by B Lewis, *The Arabs in History*, Hutchinson, London, 1950 pp. 22–3.
[5] Chapter XVI, v. 80.
[6] Philip K. Hitti, *History of the Arabs,* Macmillan, London, 1956, pp. 180 f, and pp. 501 f.

# TWO

# Mecca and the Ka'bah

Mecca, or Makkah which is its Arabic form, is one of the most renowned towns in the world, both in ancient and modern times. It stands forty-five miles from the coast of the Red Sea, and is nearly half-way between Syria in the North and the Yemen in the South.

The origin of Mecca, in the views of some authorities, appears to be obscure.[1] However, Islamic tradition ascribes its foundation to the great Prophet, Abraham, and his son Ishmael, or Ibrāhım and Ismā'īl as they are pronounced in Arabic. The tradition goes that Abraham placed his baby

*A general view of Mecca*

*Zamzam*

son, Ishmael together with his mother Hājar, in the valley where Mecca now lies.[2] It was then an isolated place. He left with them some dates and some water, and prayed to God that He might give them company and provide for them in that barren land.[3] Abraham's intention in placing Ishmael and Hājar so far away, it is believed, was to avoid the rise of domestic troubles. His wife, Sārah, began to show symptoms of jealousy after the birth of Ishmael by Abraham's slave girl, Hājar. Until then, Sarah had not begotten any children, but subsequently, she gave birth to Abraham's second son, Isaac or Ishāq as he is called in Arabic.

Hajar and Ishmael lived on the dates and water left by Abraham for some days, but, when the water was finished, Hajar began to search for water in the surrounding area, climbing up and down the hills of Safa and Marwah until the famous well of Zamzam was discovered.

Soon a group of a southern tribe, called Jurhum, who were on their way to Syria, discovered the couple and the water and decided to stay with them, as the tradition goes.[4] This is held to be a fulfilment of Abraham's prayers.

Then Ishmael grew up among the people of Jurhum and learned their Arabic tongue and their pursuits, and married within the tribe. Therefore, Ishmael and the tribes which descended from him are known as the Arabianized Arabs, in contradistinction from the original or pure Arabs of the south.

Abraham was glad that his son was settled down happily in Mecca. Occasionally he travelled and visited him. During one of these visits he informed Ishmael that God had commanded him to build a shrine in Mecca where his followers would offer their devotion to God. Ishmael helped his father build the rectangular house, henceforth known as the Ka'bah. When the building was completed Abraham proclaimed the obligation of pilgrimage to this place, where worshippers ever since have come annually to worship God.

The religion of Abraham and Ishmael, peace be upon them, prevailed in Mecca and elsewhere at the time. Those

*The Ka'bah*

who followed this religion worshipped Allah alone and did not ascribe any partner to Him. But with the passage of time and through external influences the principles of the religion of Abraham became gradually mixed up, the idolatry and pagan practices permeated it, until at the time of the birth of Muhammad every tribe and every clan had its own idols carved of wood, stone and similar materials. Allah as the supreme God remained as a vague idea. The practice of pilgrimage continued, though in a corrupted form, probably because of its economic advantages. The Ka'bah became the centre of idol worship, and was surrounded by gods which were widely recognized throughout Arabia. To the superior gods round the Ka'bah, Arabians came annually from all corners to worship and to offer sacrifices.

From this account it is clear how important Mecca was in the pre-Islamic era in the field of religion. Besides this religious significance, Mecca had another important advantage. It lay on the cross-roads of the caravan routes. When they came to perform their annual pilgrimage, the Arabs availed themselves of the opportunity and held their largest markets and fairs in the surroundings. These markets and fairs were held for quite long periods during which both worshippers and traders bought and sold their goods and products. All these aspects helped Mecca to grow as the most important commercial town in Central Arabia.

The season of pilgrimage and the markets and fairs held annually gave rise to an exceddingly significant cultural development. These events brought together members of various tribes from all corners of Arabia who conversed in a common medium. Differences of dialect were narrowed down; and the process of perfecting the Arabic tongue continued for centuries until the language reached its peak of excellence at the time of the rise of Islam.

The Ancient Arabs were extremely fond of poetry and of eloquent speeches. Poetry was the reservoir of their history and their knowledge as a whole; and the language was the art and the sacred tradition they cherished. They probably excelled all other nations in this respect. The Arabic language has many capabilities and a wide range of possibilities.

Poets and speakers who performed during these seasons delivered their efforts to the gathering attentive crowds; and tribes rose high or sank low in prestige and status on account of the performance of their spokesmen.

The dialect of Northern Arabia, with Mecca as its leading centre, became recognized as fashionable and elegant, and the model of excellence. Among its inhabitants were the masters and the undisputed authorities of the language, a significant factor adding to its commercial and religious prestige.

Among the inhabitants of Mecca, a tribe, known as Quraish, held a special distinction for the last three centuries before the rise of Islam. Quraish traced their descent from Mudar, the twelfth great-grandfather of Muhammad, who was also called Auraish. Mudar's ancestry is traced back to 'Adanān, the nineteenth great-grandfather of Muhammad, and 'Adnān's ancestry is in turn traced back to Ishmael, son of Abraham.

Until the beginning of the fourth century of the Christian era, the descendants of Ishmael never held sway in Mecca. Supremacy of the town was first held by Jurhum, the in-laws of Ishmael; but when they gradually disregarded their religious and moral code they were weakened and were defeated by another southern tribe, the Khuzā'ah. Before fleeing from Mecca the leader of the tribe of Jurhum, it is related, filled the well of Zamzam with earth and had his treasures buried in it.[5]

The failure of Jurhum constituted a blow to their related clan, the Ishmaʿilites, who henceforth were scattered all over Arabia. They remained so until the advent of Quṣayy, the fourth great-grandfather of Muhammad, who was born around the year 400 of the Christian era. Quṣayy, a man of great ability and of a forceful character, united the clans of Quraish under his own leadership. He defeated the tribe of Khuzāʿah and then assumed supremacy in Mecca.

Quṣayy introduced many reforms and established important institutions in Mecca which raised his prestige and that of his tribe extremely high. Up to his time, many of those who came to Mecca during the season of pilgrimage ran short of food but no help was extended to them. Moreover with the disappearance of the well of Zamzam, the pilgrims had suffered from acute thirst in the intense heat of Mecca. Quṣayy organized a system of collecting food by which the needy pilgrims could be fed. He also organized another system whereby water was collected from the scattered wells in the neighbourhood of Mecca, and was poured into pools near the Kaʿbah from which the pilgrims were given to drink. These two institutions were called the *Rifadah* and the *Siqayah* respectively. Quṣayy also established a council of the leaders of Quraish to consider important issues. This council henceforth became known as *al-Nadwah*, the Council of Deliberation.

The peace and order achieved by Quṣayy in Mecca, the spiritual and commercial centre of Arabia, together with the newly-established beneficial institutions, greatly enhanced the prestige of Quraish in the eyes of all the Arab tribes in the Peninsula, many of which sought to establish friendship ties and alliances with Quraish. As a result of this prestige, the caravans of Quraish travelled in the peninsula in peace and safety, which added to the wealth and prosperity of Mecca.

Quṣayy held all the posts he created together with the custodianship of the Ka'bah. Unfortunately his sons, and afterwards their descendants, disputed over these posts, and the Arab allies of Quraish were divided in their support. The sharpest split was that which occurred between Hashim, son of 'Abd Manaf, son of Quṣayy, and Hāshim's nephew, Umayyah, son of 'Abd Shams, son of 'Abd Manaf. The dispute developed to a dangerous degree and threatened the peace and prosperity of Mecca. Although the dispute ended in favour of Hashim, the wound never healed. Animosity and bitter rivalry between the clan of Hashim and the clan of Umayyah continued for many generations, and it was manifested most strikingly in the early development of the political history of Islam.[6]

In spite of these disturbances, the prestige of Quraish was maintained. It was indeed further enhanced, especially in the case of the House of Hashim, by two important events which occurred shortly before the rise of Islam. The first of these events was the excavation of the well of Zamzam by 'Abd al-Muttallib, son of Hashim.

'Abd al-Muttallib, the illustrious grandfather of Muhammad, was born to Hashim by a wife from Yathrib, an oasis north of Mecca to which reference will be made frequently later. Since the well of Zamzam had been filled with earth by the Jurhum leader before his flight from Mecca, the memory of Zamzam had faded away and its site was forgotten. With the increase in the number of pilgrims 'Abd al-Muttallib, who had inherited his father's responsibilities, suffered greatly in the preparation of water for the pilgrims, to the pleasure of his Umayyad adversaries. He was even ridiculed because he had then only one son to help him! It is related that he was guided to the site of Zamzam in his dreams; but when he dug and the water burst out it was no doubt a great relief for all the Arabs.[7]

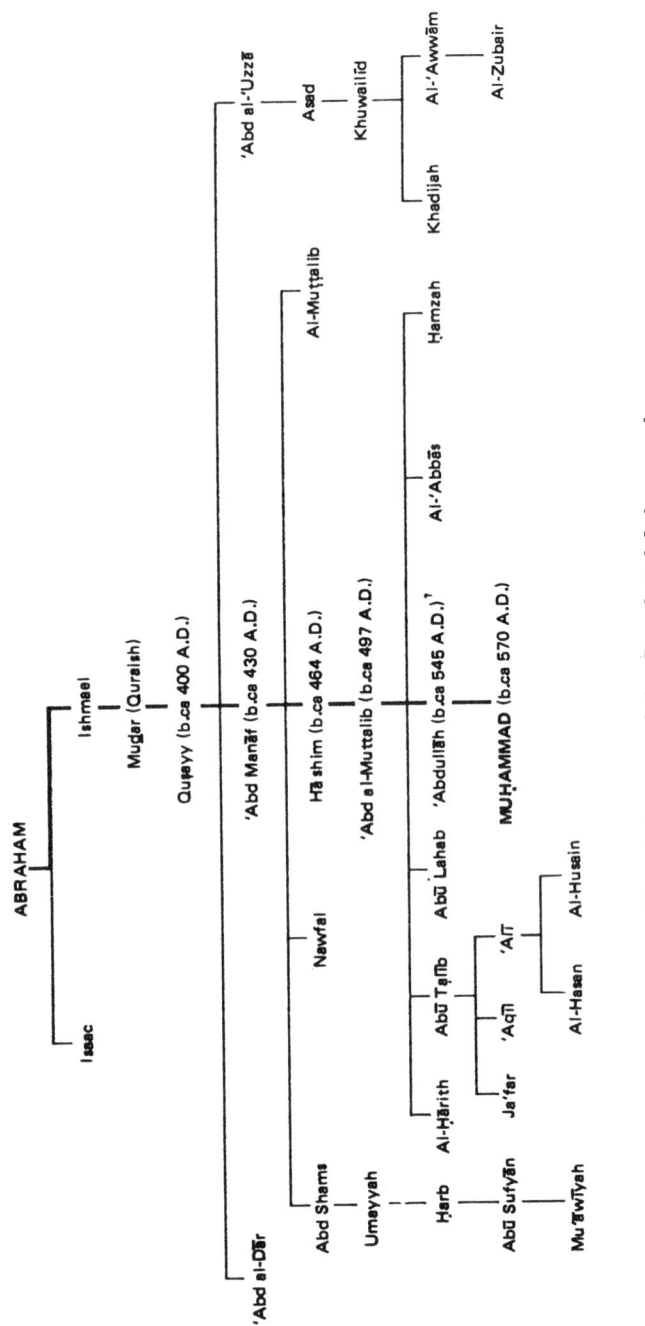

16   THE LIFE AND TEACHING OF THE PROPHET MUHAMMAD

*Lineal descent of the Prophet Muhammad*

The second, probably more important event, was the miraculous delivery of Mecca, especially the Ka'bah, from a dangerous attack by the Abyssinians, also during the time of 'Abd al-Muttallib. The Abyssinians had conquered and colonized the Yemen; but the Abyssinian leader was amazed to find all Arabia looking towards Mecca and paying annual visits to its shrine. He realized the political and economic significance of this religious leadership, and decided to divert attention from the Ka'bah by building a more elegant shrine in his capital. When his plan was unsuccessful, he launched a severe military attack on Mecca, intending to pull down the Ka'bah and to desecrate it.

The Meccans under the leadership of 'Abd al-Muttallib were helpless in front of this overwhelmingly superior power. They decided to evacuate Mecca, seeking safety in the caves of the surrounding mountains, and to leave the Sacred House, the Ka'bah, to the protection of its Lord. God did not fail them. On the eve of their march to Mecca, the aggressors were visited by dangerous diseases and many of them died. Those who survived escaped whence they had come. Mecca and the Ka'bah were saved; and the victory was hailed throughout Arabia. The aggressors had brought an elephant with them; and therefore the Arabs called the year in which the event took place 'The Year of the Elephant'.[8] It was the year 570 of the Christian era.

It was in this year that Muhammad, son of 'Abdullah, son of 'Abd al-Muttallib was born.

---

[1] B. Lewis, *The Arabs in History*, p. 34.
[2] Ibn Khaldūn, *Kitāb al-'Ibar wa-Diwān al-Mubtada' wa al-Khabar*, Cairo, 1936, Vol. I, p. 54.
[3] Qur'an, Chapter XIV, v. 37.
[4] op. cit. p. 55.
[5] Ibn Hishām, *al-Sīrah al-Nabawiyyah*, ed. by M. al-Saqqa and et al in 2 pts, Cairo 1955, pt. I, pp. 111-4.

[6] This rivalry seriously manifested itself in the civil war during the caliphate of ʿAli Ibn Abū Tālib and the persecution of the Hashimites by the Umayyads during the latter's reign, which strengthened the Shiʿa Party.
[7] op. cit. pt. I, pp. 142-7.
[8] *Ibid*, pp. 43-57.

# THREE

# Muhammad's Birth and Upbringing

'Abd al-Muttallib, son of Hashim, became the most distinguished character in Mecca for most of the early part of the sixth century of the Christian era. He continued the important services of feeding and providing water for the pilgrims started by his distinguished great-grandfather, Qusayy, and which had been best discharged by his own father, Hashim. Hashim had distinguished himself throughout Arabia for his generosity and his great ability; and had concluded treaties of friendship with Byzantium and the Ghassanids of Syria. To this nobility of origin 'Abd al-Muttallib added a highly impressive character and the privilege of the re-discovery of Zamzam.

In pre-Islamic Arabia, as in unsophisticated societies of today, chiefs derived a great prestige from the increased number of their sons. 'Abd al-Muttallib suffered in the beginning in this respect; and he therefore made a vow, in the habit of pre-Islamic Arabs, to sacrifice one of his children for the gods of the Ka'bah if he begot ten sons. When his wish was fulfilled, 'Abd al-Muttallib prepared to sacrifice his last and most beloved son, 'Abdullah. When he was seen leading his son toward Isaf and Na'ilah, two of the important idols of the Ka'bah, where he intended to offer 'Abdullah as a sacrifice, the chiefs of Mecca raised the alarm. They feared that 'Abd al-Muttallib, holding such a great position in Arabia, might thereby set a precedent for the practice of sacrificing children, which was an evil danger. On their intervention, a soothsayer was consulted, and she advised that the gods would be satisfied with the sacrifice of camels. So 'Abdullah was saved; and one hundred camels were slaughtered instead.

It is believed that Ishmael, son of Abraham, had suffered a similar experience. His father dreamt that he was commanded to sacrifice his son. When the dream was repeated, Abraham believed that it was a true command from God. He therefore took Ishmael who was then a small boy to an isolated place and prepared to cut his throat. The obedient son surrendered himself and resigned to the Divine command. Abraham, in spite of his parental sentiments, was about to cut the throat of his son when a revelation came commanding him to offer a sheep instead.[1] Thus, Ishmael was spared. It is therefore related that the Prophet Muhammad used to say, 'I am the son of al-Dhabihain',[2] that is, of the two men whose lives were about to be offered in sacrifice.

'Abdullah is reported to have been a young man of irresistible charm. The story of his deliverance lent colour to his personality. Marriageable girls became fascinated by him; it is related that they openly offered themselves to him in marriage. However it was the good fortune of Aminah, daughter of Wahb of the tribe of Zuhrah, to be destined as the wife of Abdullah and the mother of his great son ... the greatest of all those who lived on earth.

In accordance with the habit of the time, 'Abdullah lived with his bride Aminah in the house of his in-laws for three days, and then they moved together to the house of his own father 'Abd al-Muttallib, where they remained for a few weeks before 'Abdullah joined the caravan to Syria, leaving his young wife in the care of his father.

On his return journey from Syria, 'Abdullah became ill and was left behind in Yathrib to be nursed by the maternal uncles of his father. It was a disappointment for both 'Abd al-Muttallib and the young Aminah when the caravan returned to Mecca without 'Abdullah. 'Abd al-Muttallib sent for him, but before his messengers reached Yathrib, 'Abdullah was already dead.

'Abd al-Muttallib and Aminah were struck with grief. Aminah, however, had already felt the signs of conception and so the memory of 'Abdullah would be kept alive through his child. On the twelfth day of Rabi al-Awwal, (April, 570), Aminah gave birth, and it was a son. It was a great consolation to the ageing 'Abd al-Muttallib, who named the child Muhammad, and who on the seventh day of his birth held a splendid feast for which he slaughtered seven she-camels.

It was the habit of the aristocrats of Mecca to send their children away from the stifling climate of the town and trust them to wet nurses in the open air of the desert. It was the good luck of Halimah, of the tribe of Sa'd, to serve as the wet nurse of Muhammad. According to her, she and her people had suffered from poverty and shortage but when Muhammad arrived there, their valley grew green with pastures and the four years of his stay with them were marked by abundance.

When he reached the age of four, Muhammad was handed back to his mother and grandfather by Halimah. Aminah was very happy to have him back, and his grandfather lavished great care and affection on him. Muhammad was allowed to sit on the mat of 'Abd al-Muttallib in the shade of the Ka'bah, an honour denied to anyone else. 'Abd al-Muttallib foresaw a great future for his grandson.[3]

When Muhammad was six years old, his young mother took him to Yathrib to visit the maternal uncles of his grandfather. They were accompanied by Umm-Aiman, a slave girl left by his father. As 'Abdullah had died young during the life-time of his father, 'Abd al-Muttallib, he had not accumulated much wealth to leave to his own son, Muhammad, apart from this slave-girl, five camels and some sheep and goats. In Yathrib Muhammad visited the house where his father had spent the period of his illness six years previously, and was also shown his grave.

After a month's stay in Yathrib, the party began to make their way back to Mecca. When they were about twenty-two miles away from Yathrib they had to stop. Aminah fell ill and soon died. She was buried where she died under the very eyes of her young son. Muhammad had to leave behind the remains of his mother and to make the hard, long journey back to Mecca alone, only in the company of Umm-Aiman, full of grief and sorrow. It must have been a most depressing experience at his very tender age to see his mother dying, just after seeing the grave of his father who had died before he was born.

'Abd al-Muttallib, who was then in his eighties, deeply sympathized with the poor child, and lavished yet more care and affection on him. However, the old man did not live much longer. In two years' time he died, leaving Muhammad in the care of his uncle, Abu Talib, son of 'Abd al-Muttallib, who was a full brother of 'Abdullah.

None of 'Abd al-Muttallib's numerous children matched their great father in dignity or prestige. On his death they shared the posts he had held during his lifetime. Abu Talib's share was the organization of feeding the pilgrims, although in terms of wealth he was not so well-to-do. The duty of providing water for the pilgrims fell on the shoulders of his brother, al-'Abbas, a thrifty man.

Abu Talib travelled once to Syria with the caravan after his father's death. He had intended to leave Muhammad behind in Mecca, since he did not want him, at the tender age of twelve, to suffer the hardships of the long journey. He had to yield, however, to the persistent appeals of Muhammad, who he loved dearly.

No doubt the journey was a good experience for Muhammad at this early age. It must have opened his mind to the sharp differences between conditions in the fertile and prosperous Syria and those in his own barren country.

Muhammad, from his childhood, endeared himself to all those around him by his manners and virtues. The more he grew in age, the more his virtues and wisdom were recognized, until the people of Mecca conferred upon him the title of *Al-Amin*[4] which means the honest and trustworthy man. In major disputes he was appointed as an arbitrator; and his decisions were accepted by all parties concerned with satisfaction and admiration. Muhammad never took part in pagan practices prevailing in Mecca, or in the worship of idols, in spite of the displeasure this attitude had aroused among the Meccans, and in spite of the intervention of his uncle. People were impressed by Muhammad's physical charm and early mental maturity.

During his stay in the tribe of his wet-nurse in the desert, Muhammad was trained in their occupation, the tending of sheep and goats. His experience as a shepherd in the desert must also have trained him in the virtue of patience and prepared him for leadership. Under the guardianship of his uncle, moreover, Muhammad engaged himself to some degree in commercial pursuits, and had occasionally hired his labour to others in return for wages. However, by the standard prevailing in Mecca, Muhammad under the care of his uncle, led a humble but contented life.

The most important of his commercial undertakings was in association with a renowned lady, a wealthy widow held in honour and esteem in Mecca who was of beauty and good character. Her name was Khadijah, from the tribe of Asad. It was in fact on the initiative and intervention of Abu Talib that Muhammad was engaged in the trading caravan of Khadijah which was proceeding to Syria.

Muhammad was then nearly twenty-five years old and this trip was the second and last journey abroad for him. He brought back fabulous profits; and in his account of his dealings to Khadijah, he displayed the highest degree of honesty. Khadijah was amazed; and the wonderful report given to her by her slave, Maisarah, whom she had sent to accompany Muhammad and who had been closely watching Muhammad's behaviour during the journey, exercised an immense influence on her mind. Muhammad was also of rare physical charm. He had inherited the forceful and commanding, yet modest personality of his great forbears, Qusayy and Hashim. All this exerted a very favourable effect on Khadijah who, though she had earlier declined the hand of many a Meccan leader, did not hesitate to send word conveying her wish to marry Muhammad who was fifteen years younger than she.

Muhammad paid Khadijah twenty she-camels as a bridal gift, and soon the marriage was concluded. He moved into Khadijah's residence to start twenty-five years of happy married life with her. She bore him six children, Al-Qasim, Abdullah, Zainab, Ruqayyah, Umm Kulthum and Fatimah. With the exception of Fatimah, the Prophet lost all his children during his lifetime, a very hard experience which may serve as a solace for his followers in times of similar personal crises.

Although his personal virtues were a greater asset to him, Muhammad's marriage to Khadijah was an important turning point in his life. It raised his prestige higher in Mecca. It assured his livelihood, and inspired him with a greater sense of security. This enabled him to devote more time to contemplation and to thinking on the wonders of the world. He was dissatisfied with the superstitions and pagan practices prevailing in Mecca. He often wondered how his countrymen could worship man-made wooden or stone statues and figures which could in no way respond to their devotion. He disagreed with the laxity of morals and self-indulgence of the people at that time.

In his later thirties, Muhammad developed the habit of retiring to a secluded cave, away from the bustle and noise of Mecca for his solitary meditations. There he stayed for periods of varying length, sometimes reaching a month. The cave is in the mountain of *Hira'*, now called the 'Mountain of Light'. It was in this cave that the heavenly revelations began to come to him

---

[1] *Qur'ān* Chapter XXXVII, vv. 101–7.
[2] Abū Ishāq al-Nisābūrī, Qisas al-Anbiyā', Cairo 1951, p. 93.
[3] Ibn Hishām, *al-Sīrah al-Nabawiyyah*, pt. I, p. 168.
[4] *Ibid*, p. 183.

FOUR

# The Mission and Early Converts

During his retirement in the secluded cave of *Hira'*, Muhammad pondered over the wonders of the world and the secret behind them. He reflected over the events of day and night, the sun, the moon, the stars, the seas, the winds and the living creatures which come and go. Muhammad had no doubt that behind all these subtleties and regularity there was an omniscient and omnipotent Creator. But he craved for the knowledge of the nature of that Creator, his relationship to man, the highest order of creation, and of the form in which man, the intellectual creature, should express his gratitude to the benevolent Creator.

One day, while occupied in meditation in the cave, yearning for the truth, a visitor suddenly appeared, embraced him closely, and commanded him: 'Read!' The perplexed Muhammad answered that he could not read. The visitor then embraced Muhammad more closely and after releasing him, he again commanded: 'Read!' Muhammad repeated, 'I am not a reader.' The strange visitor embraced Muhammad once more and said,

> *"Read in the name of your Lord who created.*
> *He created man from clotted blood.*
> *Read, and the Lord is the most noble,*
> *He who taught by the pen,*
> *He taught man what man did not know."*[1]

( الجزء الثلاثون )

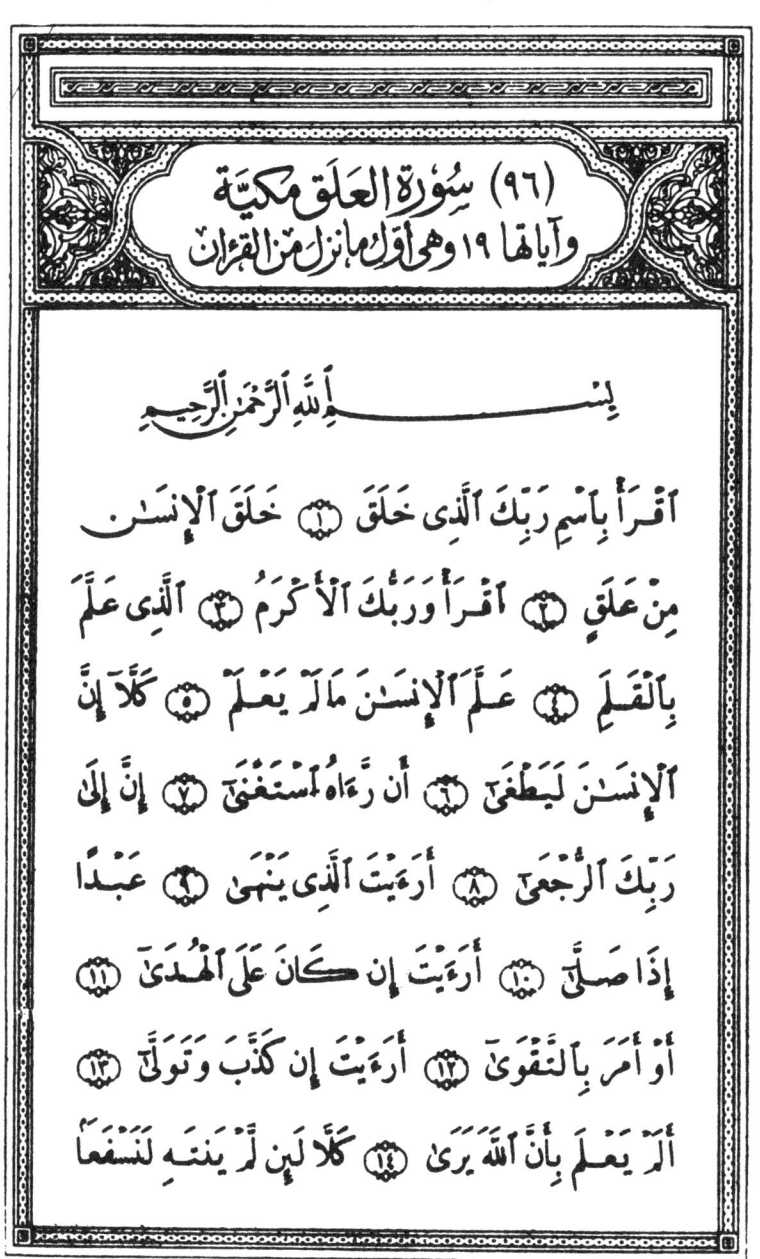

﴿٩٦﴾ سُورَةُ العَلَقِ مَكِّيَّةٌ
وآياتها ١٩ وهي أوَّلُ ما نَزَلَ مِنَ القُرآنِ

بِسْمِ اللهِ الرَّحْمٰنِ الرَّحِيمِ

اقْرَأْ بِاسْمِ رَبِّكَ الَّذِي خَلَقَ ۝ خَلَقَ الْإِنْسَانَ مِنْ عَلَقٍ ۝ اقْرَأْ وَرَبُّكَ الْأَكْرَمُ ۝ الَّذِي عَلَّمَ بِالْقَلَمِ ۝ عَلَّمَ الْإِنْسَانَ مَا لَمْ يَعْلَمْ ۝ كَلَّا إِنَّ الْإِنْسَانَ لَيَطْغَىٰ ۝ أَنْ رَآهُ اسْتَغْنَىٰ ۝ إِنَّ إِلَىٰ رَبِّكَ الرُّجْعَىٰ ۝ أَرَأَيْتَ الَّذِي يَنْهَىٰ ۝ عَبْدًا إِذَا صَلَّىٰ ۝ أَرَأَيْتَ إِنْ كَانَ عَلَى الْهُدَىٰ ۝ أَوْ أَمَرَ بِالتَّقْوَىٰ ۝ أَرَأَيْتَ إِنْ كَذَّبَ وَتَوَلَّىٰ ۝ أَلَمْ يَعْلَمْ بِأَنَّ اللهَ يَرَىٰ ۝ كَلَّا لَئِنْ لَمْ يَنْتَهِ لَنَسْفَعًا

*Earliest part of Qur'anic Revelation (first 5 verses of Chapter 96, appearing in the three lines on the top)*

The vision then disappeared, and Muhammad was extremely shaken. The visitor had spoken of interesting topics, God, His creation, reading and knowledge; but being unfamiliar with earlier prophetic calls and experiences, Muhammad, who was then forty, did not realize the nature of the call. He felt as if he were suffering from fever. He rushed home, went to bed and asked his wife to cover him.

Khadijah was a very wise and understanding woman. For the last fifteen years during which she had been living with her noble husband, her admiration of his wisdom and her appreciation of his virtues had continuously grown. She therefore believed that the strange visitor in the cave had not come with a malevolent purpose, although she could not realize fully his nature. She, therefore, left Muhammad in bed and went to consult her ageing paternal cousin who was familiar with the old scriptures.

Before Khadijah returned with the good tidings that the visitor was probably the angel who had descended with heavenly revelations to earlier prophets, Muhammad had already been assured of this through another contact with the supernatural. During this second experience many of Muhammad's problems were solved, many of his queries were answered, and his fears and doubts were removed. He established familiarity with the supernatural messenger and ever after he referred to him as 'My brother Gabriel'.[2]

Muhammad looked forward to further calls; and after a fairly long interval, Gabriel came down and revealed to him that he had been chosen by God as His last Messenger to deliver to mankind His message and to invite them to the truth. It was no doubt an extremely hard task, but it was the noblest message and was of the greatest consequence.

Muhammad began to plan the method of discharging his duties. Before proceeding to consider how he did it and how the people responded to his invitation, it is now convenient to discuss the main features of his message at this stage.

There was nothing peculiar in Muhammad's prophetic call. He merely claimed to have been one, and the last, in the series of the noble messengers of God which began with Adam. None of the men in that series, including Christ, as Muslims believe, claimed and supernatural elements in his nature, although all of them asserted their contacts with the supernatural. They were ordinary men, but of the highest degree of integrity, ability, intelligence and honesty.

The basic foundation of the message of all those messengers or prophets was the belief that everything in the world was planned or pre-determined in eternity, created in time, and sustained and continued by a righteous Creator, God, Whom, Muhammad called *Allah,* to Whom we owe everything, and Who deserves alone all our gratitude, all our worship and devotion. He is one, omnipotent and omniscient, and to ascribe to Him anything that makes Him resemble creatures, amounts to disbelief in Him. From the point of view of Islam, therefore, it is blasphemy to call Him father or to ascribe sonship or partnership to Him. It is impiety to prostrate, to kneel or to bow in front of any beside Him.

In addition to the basic belief in Allah, the Almighty, men should observe in their behaviour, propriety and righteousness. There will be rewards for those who comply with the recognized moral code; and the unrepenting transgressor will have to suffer. Rewards and punishment will take place when all mankind are resurrected and brought to account by God Whose knowledge reaches the depth of the hearts of men. The abode of the righteous will be Paradise, and Hell is the doom for the evildoers.

Muhammad's moral code at that stage consisted of insistence on the universally recognized virtues, and avoidance of what are considered as vices. It was virtuous to respect the rights of others, to be truthful, to be honest, to fulfil pledges and to keep promises, to honour parents, to be helpful to all relatives, neighbours, orphans and slaves, especially to those who need help. On the other hand, it was sin to encroach upon others, to despise them, to injure them, to cheat them or to take advantage of the weakness of the underprivileged.

A fundamental part of the teaching of Muhammad was the absolute equality of mankind. Every individual, man or woman is directly and equally responsible to God; and when no biological factors justify any differences, no classification is admissible.

Besides the basic belief in God and in the Divine judgement after Resurrection, the adherents of Islam, who became known as Muslims, are to hold all Prophets who came before Muhammad in honour and respect. There were many of them; each was sent to guide his own community. The basic teaching of them all was the same; but the guidance they gave in matters of practice varied in accordance with the needs of time and locality. Muhammad, the Seal of them, brought the same faith. His message, however, is universal, not limited to his people, the Arabs alone; and his guidance is held to be suitable for all times and all environments.

While all Messengers should be held in esteem, the Prophethood of twenty-five of them should be specifically acknowledged. Besides Muhammad and his great grandfathers Ishmael, Abraham, Noah and Adam, they are: Enoch, Hud, Shu'aib, Salih, Ezekiel, Isaac, Jacob, David, Solomon, Job, Joseph, Moses, Aaron, Zachariah, John, Jesus, Elias, Elisha, Jonah and Lot.

Muhammad received the Divine message through the direct revelation by Gabriel, and occasionally through other ways such as dreams where information was imparted to his mind and he was convinced that it was Divine knowledge and not passing whims. Some of the revelation was given in specific words to be preserved and repeated as revealed; and other parts of it were just ideas or information which the Prophet put into his own words. The first category became known as the Qur'an, and the second was called *Hadith* or Tradition.

Muhammad had to begin preaching his faith in the community of Mecca where he lived. But he realized how radically his teaching differed from the basic beliefs and practices prevailing in Mecca and throughout Arabia. His religion struck at the roots of the heathen religion, and would bring to destruction the foundations of the aristocratic society of Mecca. He therefore had to move slowly and cautiously. If he began preaching the new faith publicly and openly, his religion would be smothered to death in its infancy. Muhammad therefore decided to preach his new religion privately; and first approached selected individuals who were close to him and whom he could trust.

Muhammad's personal charms and his persuasive method gained him a few devoted adherents. The first to follow his faith was his wife who had been through all his experiences for the last fifteen years. She had no hesitation, and she was followed by Zaid Ibn Harithah, a former slave boy, purchased and emancipated by Muhammad and adopted as his son, in the pre-Islamic fashion. He was therefore called Zaid Ibn Muhammad. Adoption was later prohibited in Islam; and Zaid was called after his real father.

A few years earlier Muhammad, sympathizing with the condition of his uncle Abu Talib, who had many children to care for, offered to take one of his sons, 'Ali, to bring up in Khadijah's house. It is not unlikely that the adoption of Zaid and the taking over of the responsibility of bringing up 'Ali were related to the loss by Khadijah and Muhammad of their two sons in their childhood.

One evening, 'Ali, who was then about ten, saw the noble couple, performing prayers, the early form of Islamic devotion which, towards the end of the Meccan period, developed into the form of the five daily prayers. 'Ali enquired, and the Prophet informed him of the new faith and invited him to embrace it. By then Muhammad had given a formula to be recited by new converts as an expression of their acceptance of the new religion which he called Islam. It was 'I certify that there is no God but Allah and certify that Muhammad is the messenger of Allah.' 'Ali promised to consult his father, but the following morning he came forward and declared his acceptance of the faith of Islam. He said, 'Allah did not consult Abu Talib when He created me; why should I consult my father when I want to worship Allah.'[3]

Another distinguished early convert was Abu Bakr Ibn Abu Quhafah from the tribe of Taim. He was an intimate friend of Muhammad, and two years younger than he. He was a trader of considerable success, and of wide renown for his generosity and wisdom. He was acknowledged as an authority on the genealogies of the Arab tribes; and he was destined to become later the first Caliph in Islam.

---

[1]Qur'ān, Chapter IXC, vv. 1–5 Ibn Hisham, *al-Sirah al-Nabawiyyah*, pt. I, pp. 336–7.
[2]His Arabic version is *Jibril*.
[3]Emile Dermenghem, *The Life of Mahomet*, Routledge, London 1930, pp. 69–70.

# FIVE

# Reaction of Mecca to the Mission

The first Muslim group consisted of Muhammad, his wife Khadijah, his adopted son, Zaid, his cousin Ali and his faithful friend Abu Bakr. The Prophet continued his efforts to spread the faith secretly. His method was persuasion and could not be coercion. All he had to do was to reveal the truth; and it was left to the individual to choose one way or the other.

The principles of equality and justice in Islam, and the moral ideals of the new religion appealed most to the lower strata of society. Thus a number of slaves of Byzantine or Abyssinian origin were among the early Muslims. Women also were less hesitant. In addition to this, a number of Meccan dignitaries through the efforts of Abu Bakr joined the circle of Islam early, and they were all reckoned among the most illustrious Companions of the Prophet.

Although the Prophet pursued his efforts cautiously, the advent of his religion soon became known. The leaders of Mecca were shocked. They could never think of their idols being humiliated, or their old habits being criticized. Their prestige and superiority were based on the esteem accorded to the gods of whom they were the custodians; and their favourable economic position was built on that religious prerogative. Moreover, they could not agree with the principle of equality, or imagine that their slaves and labourers and women could have independent personalities like themselves. They could not, therefore, tolerate Muhammad's religion, although so far they had held him in great honour and respect.

The people of Mecca, dissuaded everyone from following Muhammad, and applied the hardest pressure on those who had joined him. The lot of the slaves and the weaker individuals who embraced Islam were very miserable. They were exposed to severe sufferings and hardships, but none yielded an inch. An atmosphere of tension prevailed throughout the town; and Muhammad and his followers had to go to a hiding place when they wanted to offer their devotion to God.

At this stage there was no point in concealing the new faith any more, and Muhammad no longer hesitated to declare his message publicly. He had already had a Qur'anic revelation that he should do so.[1] He climbed the Mount of Safa and called loudly the names of the clans of Quraish. People rushed to him, and when they had gathered he said, 'If inform you that cavalry is attacking you from behind that mountain, would you believe me?' They answered, 'You have always been truthful.' Then he said, 'I have come to warn you of a severe punishment.' 'By Allah, besides Whom there is no god, I am indeed His messenger to you specially and to the world at large. By Allah you will die as you sleep, and will be resurrected as you awake. By Allah you will be called to account for all your acts. You will be well rewarded for your good deeds and punished for your sins. Indeed it will be Paradise forever or Hell forever.'[2]

Voices rose against Muhammad, severest among them being that of Abu Lahab, one of his paternal uncles, who shouted, 'Woe unto you Muhammad! Is that what you have gathered us for?' Then he added, turning to the leaders of the Quraishite clans, 'Capture him now before he can build up a strong following.'[3]

The gathering however dispersed in confusion, and the public declaration of the new faith sharpened the opposition against it. The influential clans in Mecca formed a league of opposition against the clans of Hashim and al-Muttalib, which were led by Abu Talib. Abu Talib was not himself a Muslim; but because of clan loyalties and obligations, and also because of his love for Muhammad, he declared his protection of him up to the end.

The opposition leaders appealed to Abu Talib a number of times to persuade Muhammad to give up his claims, but Abu Talib disregarded the appeal. When they threatened strong action against the clans under his leadership, then Abu Talib spoke to Muhammad who replied, 'My Uncle, even if they place the sun in my right hand, and place the moon in my left hand, I shall never give up this matter until it prevails or I die.' Tears came into the eyes of Muhammad who turned and went away. Abu Talib, who was moved by his determination called him, and said, 'Go and say what you want...I shall never let you down.':

It became then an issue between two camps in Mecca, the small group of Hashim and al-Muttallib under the leadership of Abu Talib and the large opposition group of allies led by 'Amr Ibn Hisham, whom Muhammad nicknamed Abu Jahl, 'Father of Ignorance'.

The opposition, in their efforts to embarrass Muhammad, demanded that he should produce as evidence miracles of a foolish character. They asked him to make Mecca an arable land with rivers and orchards, to bring down his God and the angles and to raise the dead and let them talk to them.[5]

If the Meccans were sincere in their attitude, there could be no better evidence for Muhammad's doctrine of God than nature itself which spoke of the Creator and His divinity.

There could be no better evidence of the truthfulness of the message of Muhammad than the Qur'an. Muhammad asserted that the words of the Qur'an were not written by him. They were the words of God and were, therefore, in an order of eloquence inimitable by man. On the other hand, the Meccans were acknowledged the best authors and authorities of the language.

Muhammad challenged the Meccans to produce something similar in eloquence and excellence to the Qur'an, if they denied its divine character. The Meccans failed badly in the challenge, and to cover their embarrassment they accused Muhammad of being a magician.[6] But, how could a magician who was illiterate produce such a book far beyond the attainment of the leaders of Mecca, a book which accurately related ancient events[7] and correctly foretold future happenings?[8] Could an imposter living in Mecca in the seventh century and opposed by nearly all his community produce such a clear and simple system of faith, such a perfect system of moral conduct, and such a complex, but coherent, consistent, complete and comprehensive system of legislation, all embodied in a book?

Nothing but material considerations and the blind love of the inherited beliefs and traditions prompted the hostile attitude adopted by the people of Mecca towards Muhammad. They had known him for forty years before he declared his mission, and they had acknowledged his wisdom and integrity, and recognized him as the most honest and truthful man among them.

In spite of their vehement opposition, the adversaries of Muhammad, who became known as infidels or unbelievers, were moved by the effect of the Qur'an whenever they heard it recited. Their women and children under the cover of darkness at night used to gather round the house of Abu Bakr to hear him recite the Qur'an. But the conceited aristocrats of Mecca feared the loss of their prestige and privileges if the 'democratic' ideals of Islam flourished. In their attempt to smother the new faith, they turned the ordinary folk from the right path and subjected those who upheld the truth to severe torture. They did not hesitate to apply the most appalling methods of persecution against the believers. Each tribe undertook to deal with its own members who became Muslims. They tortured them by fire and by heated rods of iron. The bodies of their victims were chained, exposed naked to the heat of the burning midday sun, and they were made to lie with heavy rocks placed on their chests. Some of them died and some lost their sight, but none gave in. Muhammad, of course, was not spared. Abu Lahab, who against the tribal law, joined the opposition camp, was exceedingly aggressive. He happened to be a neighbour of Muhammad, and the harm inflicted by him was unrelenting. The Prophet was mocked and insulted, and entrails of slaughtered animals were thrown on him. He would once have been nearly strangled had it not been for the timely intervention of Abu Bakr. He set Muhammad free from the hands of the unbelieving aggressors and said, 'Would you kill a man merely because he says, "Allah is my Lord, while he brought you evidence from your Lord"?'[9] The Prophet, however, defeated the unbelievers by his most striking clemency. He never reacted in an angry mood, but he always said, 'God, forgive their sins and guide them in the right path.'[10]

[1] Qur'ān, Chapter XV, v. 94.
[2] Muhammad Husain Haikal, *Hayāt Muhammad*, Cairo, 1956, p. 142.
[3] *Ibid*, p. 142.
[4] Ibn Hishām, *al-Sīrah al-Nabawiyyah*, pt. I, p. 226.
[5] Qur'ān, Chapter XVI, vv. 90–3 and Chapter VI, vv. 109–11.
[6] Qur'ān, Chapters VI, v. 7; XI, v. 7; XXI, v. 3, XXXVII, 15; XLIII, 30; XLVI, 7; LIV, 2; LXI, 6; LXXIV, 24; XXXVIII, 4.
[7] Namely the stories of the past nations and earlier Prophets.
[8] E.g., Chapter XXX, 1–6, where the defeat of the Persians by the Byzanties was predicted. It is related that the verses were revealed when the Meccans rejoiced at the defeat of the Byzantines who were monotheists like Muhammad, by the Persians who were in a way polytheists like the Meccans.
[9] Ibn Hishām, *al-Sīrah al-Nabawiyyah*, pt. I, p. 290.
[10] *Matn al-Bukhārī*, al-Halabi Press, Cairo, n.d., Vol. II, p. 262.

SIX

# Persecution and Endurance

Muslims sustained untold torture at the hands of the unbelievers of Mecca with patience. They had relief in the company of the Prophet whom they loved more than themselves. But the Prophet was exceedingly perturbed by their sufferings. He therefore gave them permission to leave Mecca and emigrate to Abyssinia where they could enjoy the protection of its just Ruler, the Negus. Sixteen Companions left, eleven men and five women, including 'Uthman Ibn 'Affan and his wife Ruqaiyah, the first daughter of Muhammad.

Abu Bakr had decided to go, but on the way he was dissuaded from doing so by an eminent Arab chief of the desert[1] who was an ally of Mecca. The chief intervened with the opposition party, and they agreed to abstain from torturing Abu Bakr, who would be under his protection, provided that Abu Bakr would not raise his voice while reading the Qur'an. Only those who could not leave Mecca, like the slaves, remained behind.

Although this emigration to Abyssinia was associated with the persecution, the Prophet may have also expected that the news of the advent of the new religion would spread. It is reported that a Christian delegation from Najran in the Yemen, who heard of Islam as a result of this trip, came forward and declared their conversion to the new faith.[2]

The emigrants had to leave Mecca unobserved by their torturers. One of the emigrating women when on her way outside Mecca suddenly came across one of the fiercest of the opponents of Islam, whose name, nevertheless, later became closely associated with the glory of Islam. He was 'Umar Ibn al-Khattab who hitherto had been a formidable adversary of Muhammad. In the course of the argument with this woman, 'Umar came to know of the conversion of his own sister Fatimah, and her husband. He was instantly perturbed and became infuriated and rushed to his sister and brother-in-law. He attacked his sister in a harsh manner, but he was amazed by her firmness. He lowered his head for a while and then said, 'Let me hear what you have been murmuring.' The Qur'anic reader who was at the time in Fatimah's house, came out of his hiding and recited the initial part of Taha, Chapter Twenty-one of the Qur'an. 'Umar's heart began to soften. Without demur, he requested to be shown the way to the Prophet; and a harsh aggressor became a staunch supporter.

It is related that 'Umar brought the number of Muslims to forty. His conversion is said to have taken place in the sixth year of Muhammad's mission.

'Umar's conversion, of which he made no secret, was a great victory for Islam, and constituted a supreme blow to the unbelievers. 'Umar's personal courage and prestige and his clan's affiliations accorded him a special protection, and the shock his conversion caused the unbelievers resulted in a temporary amelioration in the persecution of the Muslims under them.

Seeing that Muhammad was growing in strength the unbelievers resorted to diplomatic methods in settling their disputes with him. They offered compromises, including giving Muhammad power in Mecca, paying him half the wealth of the town, and sharing in the worship of his God if he ceased abusing their idols. But Muhammad was completely devoted to his mission, and was not in the least motivated by personal ambitions. Therefore none of their offers could appeal to him.

When all their offers were rejected, the unbelievers held a special meeting to decide what to do with Muhammad who was so steadfast in his faith. They had to take into consideration, however, the attitude of the clans of Hashim and al-Muttallib who were not by any means willing to withdraw their protection from him. If he were killed there would be no peace in Mecca forever.

In order to bring the clans of Hashim and al-Muttallib to their senses, the unbelievers decided that these two clans should be boycotted by all the other clans of Quraish who formed the grand alliance of opposition. They should not sell to them or buy from them, and there should be no intermarriage with them. A document declaring this boycott was hung on the wall of the Ka'bah.

As a result of this boycott the clans of Hashim and al-Muttallib, under the leadership of Abu Talib, were isolated for nearly three years, during which they suffered increasingly, but were never prepared to give up Muhammad. When the leaders of the infidel alliance realized the ineffectiveness of the boycott as a result of the determination of Muhammad's clans, which invited the sympathy of some of the opposition members, they gave up. The embargo was lifted and the document of boycott hanging on the wall of the Ka'bah was torn down.

The end of the boycott, however, did not mean that the persecution was stopped or even mitigated. On the contrary, it continued with greater severity and intensity.

Meanwhile the emigrants to Abyssinia were back in Mecca after three months of absence. They had heard of 'Umar's conversion and the negotiations over compromises between the Prophet and Quraish; and they thought that an amicable settlement had been reached or was about to be reached. By the time they arrived in Mecca, however, the boycott of Muhammad's clans had started, and the persecution of

Muslims who could not emigrate was greatly intensified. Abu Bakr bought a number of Muslim slaves from their masters at fantastic prices in order to deliver them from the savage persecution. He emancipated them all for the sake of Allah.

Seeing the situation, the disappointed emigrants returned to Abyssinia taking many others with them. The emigrating party this time consisted of about eighty-three men and eighteen women. The Prophet was left behind in the enclosure of Abu Talib, together with the members of the boycotted clans. Muslims who could not emigrate continued in their suffering and hardship.

When the Meccans heard of this emigration they feared its consequences. Therefore they sent a delegation to the Negus requesting him to deliver it to those emigrants who had deviated from the established traditions of Mecca. The ambassadors of Mecca, led by 'Amr Ibn al 'As, had taken with them valuable presents for the Negus and his advisers. The Negus, who was impressed by the leader of the Muslim emigrants, Ja'far Ibn Abu Talib, and by the latter's description of the religion of Islam, refused to hand the Muslims over to their adversaries. The Meccan emissaries thus failed badly, and the Muslim refugees remained safe under the protection of the Abyssinian Ruler until they joined the Prohet some years later in Madinah.

Shortly after the end of the boycott the Prophet met with two grievous misfortunes. His beloved and faithful wife who had lent him so much support died. Very soon afterwards, Abu Talib to whom Muhammad owed his own protection, followed. These two misfortunes took place in the tenth year of Muhammad's mission. The Prophet called it the 'Year of Sorrow'.

The loss of these two faithful and influential supporters of his led the unbelievers to harden their opposition to Muhammad, who was therefore forced to seek support elsewhere.

Accompanied by Zaid, his emancipated slave, Muhammad travelled to Ta'if, about a hundred miles south of Mecca, which is famous for its orchards and its kind climate. The main tribe of the inhabitants of Ta'if, Thaqif, was a traditional rival of the tribe of Quraish of Mecca. Muhammad called on the leaders of Thaqif and requested them to extend their protection to him and invited them to embrace Islam. Muhammad was misunderstood by Thaqif, and the reception they accorded him was outrageous. Not only did they reject his faith and refuse to extend their protection to him, but he was expelled from the town, chased and stoned by their slaves and children.

Now Muhammad's re-entry into Mecca became a problem. He had hoped that his mission to Thaqif would be a secret unknown to his opponents in Mecca. The Thaqif leaders refused to conceal it. On the contrary they had induced their slaves, their women and children to chase Muhammad out of their town shouting abuse and throwing stones at him. In this disgraceful manner the people of Thaqif bade farewell to Muhammad. Nobody realized that in a matter of a few years they would be conquered by him and would all bow to his authority.[3]

It is related that while Muhammad was bleeding as a result of the stones thrown at him, it was suggested to him that he should curse his attackers and call down severe punishment on them, but he replied, 'No, I wish them to be spared. They may beget children who will worship God alone and ascribe no partnership to him.'[4]

Muhammad, however, managed somehow to re-enter Mecca safely. Sympathizing with Muhammad's misfortunes, a chivalrous Meccan from amongst the leaders of the opposition extended protection to him in the Arabian manner, and secured for him permission of re-entry.[5]

Muhammad returned to Mecca to continue in loneliness the hardship of the Meccan persecution, deprived of the company of Khadijah and the support of Abu Talib. He then proposed to 'A'ishah, the young daughter of Abu Bakr. Meanwhile he married Sawdah, daughter of Zam'ah, a widow who had earlier emigrated with her late husband to Abyssinia. There could be no better consolation for her.

In these dark days Muhammad never ceased to assure his persecuted followers of ultimate victory and of their becoming in the near future the heirs of the thrones of the surrounding states. At this juncture, consolation was given to Muhammad in the form of his miraculous night journey to the mosque of Jerusalem, known as *isra'*, and his ascent known as *mi'raj*. It was during that journey, it is believed, that the five daily prayers were established in their present form.[6]

The Meccans started a campaign against Muhammad abroad. Although this campaign spread the news about the faith and aroused curiosity and interest in it, it was not without its adverse effect on the efforts of Muhammad during the pilgrimage season. When he approached the tribes who came to Mecca on pilgrimage, they were not prepared to listen to him.

In spite of all these setbacks, Muhammad's confidence and perseverance never decreased. His persecuted followers never gave up hope, although life that year must have become extremely hard for the small community of Islam. Abu Talib and Khadijah had died, and their Muslim brethren were away in Abyssinia. Muhammad's mission to Ta'if was not only a complete failure, but had caused the infidels to further harden their persecution, since Muhammad had sought protection from their rivals in Ta'if. Muhammad's attempts among the pilgrims over the previous years had also been unsuccessful.

In the thickness of this darkness, however, glimpses of success began to appear. Six pilgrims from Yathrib, a town two hundred and eighty miles north of Mecca, accepted the faith of Islam and promised to return the next season with a larger number of believers.

---

[1] *He was Malik Ibn al-Dughunnah who was then the chief of an alliance between three clans including his own.*
[2] *It is said that they were from Najran, Yemen, and when they heard about the Prophet in Abyssinia they came to Mecca and embraced Islam despite the dissuasion of Abu Jahl, (al-Sirah al-Nabawiyyah, pt. 1, pp. 391–2).*
[3] *Infra, p.* 96.
[4] *Matn al-Bukhārī, Vol. II, pp.* 214–5.
[5] *He was al-Mutcin Ibn ⁹Adiyy.*
[6] *Matn al-Bukhārī, Vol. II, pp.* 326–8.

# SEVEN

# Yathrib (Madinah), and Glimpses of Success

Yathrib was an oasis of abundant water and highly fertile soil. Besides numerous groves of date palms, there were vineyards, and lemons, peaches, bananas and orange trees.

The richness of the soil of Yathrib and the abundance of its water had invited emigrants both from north and south in ancient times. When the Jews were driven out of Palestine by the Greeks and the Romans in the early days, they scattered and some of them settled down in northern Arabian oases where they introduced organized agriculture and established towns. Three of these Jewish tribes settled down in Yathrib exploiting its natural wealth and assuming supremacy over its indigenous pagan Arabs. They were the tribes of *Quraidhah, Nadir,* and *Qainuqa'*.

When, on the other hand, the famous dam of *Ma'rib* in the Yemen was destroyed, many southern tribes emigrated to the north. Some of these immigrant tribes established powerful kingdoms such as the *Ghassanids* in Syria, and the *Lakhmids* in Iraq, and the kingdom of *Kindah* in Central Arabia.

Two of these Arabian tribes settled down in Yathrib alongside the Jewish tribes whom they served as labourers. They were the tribes of *Khazraj* and the tribe of *Aws*. Soon these energetic emigrant Arabs gathered force, and eventually deprived the Jews of their power, taking over their forts in the town and building new ones in the Southern Arabian style. This took place about the middle of the sixth century A.D.

It was into a clan of the Khazraj tribe, called al-Najjar, that Hashim, son of 'Abd Manaf, had married; and it was through this marriage that 'Abd al-Muttallib, grandfather of Muhammad, was born. It was also with this clan that 'Abdullah, Muhammad's father, has stayed during his illness, and it was in their graveyard that 'Abdullah was laid to rest.

When the Jews were humiliated at the hands of the Arabs in Yathrib, they thought that they could only flourish if they created disunity and ill feeling between the two Arabian groups. The Jewish intrigues gradually built up mistrust and mutual fear between the Khazrajites and the Awsites, and eventually skirmishes began to take place. The Jews, encouraged by their success, added fuel to the flames and the feuds developed into major wars, with each tribe bringing in allies on its side. One of their most serious engagements was the Battle of Bu'ath which is believed to have taken place in 617 A.D. In that battle, the Khazrajites inflicted heavy losses on their adversaries; but somehow the Awsites by resolute determination managed to inflict a crushing defeat on their enemies.

In the subsequent years, an uneasy atmosphere prevailed in the town. Nothing could obliterate the bitter memories on both sides. The enmity was manifested in complete physical separation between the two parties. Neither of the two groups would sell to or buy from the other. There was no longer intermarriage between them. Each tribe even had its own market and its own currency.

Some of the wise men, however, began to think of creating a form of unity between the Awsites and the Khazrajites; and they thought that the best way was by the appointment of a common chief who commanded the respect of both sides. Their eyes centred on one 'Abdullah Ibn Ubayy Ibn Salul from the tribe of Khazraj.

'Abdullah, however, was not the man of the hour. He was lacking in honesty and in character. The Man of the Hour was the one who was being persecuted in Mecca, and who was to unite, not only the Khazrajites and the Awsites, not only all the Arabs, Bedouins and civilized tribes, but all Arabs and non-Arabs, under the banner of his new faith and the guidance of God. The Qur'an reads in this connexion:

*"And (God) has united their hearts (under your leadership). If you spent all (the wealth) that is on earth, you could not have united them; but Allah has united them. Allah is Great and Wise indeed!"*[1]

Muhammad, since 610 A.D., had been active in Mecca trying to persuade its inhabitants and those who called there on pilgrimage or for other purposes, to accept his faith. His success among the Meccans was very limited; and outsiders whom he invited, hesitated, partly as a result of the propaganda launched against him by the chiefs of Mecca. Muhammad's determination, however, was never shaken; and in the tenth year of the advent of his mission, namely 620 A.D., three years after the battle of Bu'ath, six pilgrims from Yathrib, from the tribe of Khazraj, accepted his faith as related above.[2]

This was perhaps Muhammad's first major success, and it took place in the year which followed the Year of Sorrow in which he had lost his uncle and his wife, and in which he suffered great humiliation at Ta'if. The six converts from Yathrib were so enthusiastic that they promised to undertake spreading the faith in their own town, which they actually did. During the following season of pilgrimage five of them returned with another seven new Muslims, including two women.

The party this time included three members of the tribe of Aws. At a place called *al-'Aqabah* they held a secret meeting with the Prophet during which they confessed their faith in Allah alone and undertook not to steal or encroach on the property of others, not to commit adultery, not to kill their children, not to promote scandals, and not to disobey any divine command. This agreement is known as the 'First Pledge of 'Aqabah'.

When the party returned, the Prophet sent with them Mus'ab Ibn 'Umair, one of his Meccan followers who was blind, to teach them the Qur'an and to lead them in prayers. Mus'ab was very successful in his mission. In spite of some opposition in the beginning, the leaders of the two major Arab tribes embraced the Islamic faith, and in a very short period the word Islam was on everybody's lips.

The party of pilgrims from Yathrib in the following season, in the year 622 A.D. included seventy-five Muslims, among whom there were two women. This Muslim group arranged a secret meeting with Muhammad at the same meeting place of the former year, al-'Aqabah. By then, these Muslims had realized that Muhammad was destined to be their saviour. They also appreciated the hardships suffered by him and his followers in Mecca. They therefore invited him to emigrate and stay with them, and pledged themselves to protect him as if he were one of them. The Prophet accepted their invitation, and this was the first step in the famous event known as the Emigration or *Hijrah*.

It is no wonder that Islam could spread more easily in Yathrib than in Mecca. The Arabs of Yathrib did not suffer from the obstacles which handicapped the Meccans. The latter were the protectors of the world of heathenism, and the custodians of the leading idols to which peoples from all corners came annually to pay homage. This brought them prestige and wealth along with other advantages. This situation, moreover, brought about a social structure in Mecca which was incompatible with the democratic ideals of Islam. In Yathrib, on the other hand, the position was quite different. Its Arab inhabitants who came originally from the civilized nation of Saba', had no claim to a religious or cultural leadership. Their endemic internal feuds worked on by the Jews had prepared them to accept such pacific ideas and ideals as were preached by Muhammad. In addition, their contiguity with the Jews, who had been critical and contemptuous of the pagan practices of the Arabs, had familiarized them with the idea of heavenly revelations, and had, in a way, made them less resistant to accepting prophetic missions. It is even related that the Jews used to mention that an Arabian Prophet would come, and would eliminate heathenism and establish the faith in the unity of God.[3]

The last agreement between Muhammad and the Muslims of Yathrib became known as 'The Second Pledge of 'Aqabah', and although all precautions were taken, the news somehow reached the ears of Quraish. They questioned some of the Yathribite pilgrims, but they happened to ask unbelievers who did not know of the meeting. The Prophet, however, did not lose time. He advised his Meccan followers to emigrate to Yathrib, and they left Mecca secretly, individually or in small groups, and on arrival they became guests of their fellow Muslims in Yathrib. Their hosts offered them all help and hospitality. Those who emigrated were henceforth called the *Muhajirun*, that is, emigrants and the Muslims of Yathrib became known as the *Ansar*, the supporters.

Some non-Muslim authors[4] claim that Muhammad's intention in sending his Meccan followers to Yathrib in advance, was to ensure his own protection, because he did not have enough confidence in the pledge made to him by the Ansar of Yathrib. We feel disinclined to accept this proposition. The Ansar gave Muhammad an Arabian pledge on which he could confidently count. Among the ancient Arabs, failure to honour a pledge of protection was unthinkable. However, the number of Muhajirun was only about seventy. How could Muhammad rely on protection from such a band of fugitives, if their hosts should prove hostile or insincere? It would have been much wiser to remain at home in Mecca under the protection of the Hashimite clans and the clan of Nawfal, the latter having ensured his safe re-entry to Mecca on his return from Ta'if. A more likely interpretation of Muhammad's advising his Meccan adherents to emigrate to Yathrib before him is this. He probably feared that, if he departed first from Mecca, the plan of emigration would soon become known to his adversaries, who, enraged by his escape, would undoubtedly intensify beyond all proportion their persecution of his followers, and their escape to Yathrib would become unlikely. The delay in his own departure was obviously much wiser in the circumstances. It also speaks much for the Prophet's concern about his companions that he gave regard to their safety before his own.

[1] *Chapter VIII, v. 63.*
[2] *Supra, pp. 43-44.*
[3] *Qur'ān, II, v. 89.*
[4] *Professor B. Lewis, The Arabs in History, p. 41, thinks that this was partly in order that Muhammad would not arrive as a lonely outlaw but as a leader with a definite status.*

# EIGHT

## The Hijrah

Quraish of Mecca somehow suspected that Muhammad had arranged to go and settle in Yathrib. His followers, one after another, disappeared from Mecca, apparently having gone to Yathrib. The leaders of Mecca therefore held an emergency meeting in the house of Qusayy to consider what should be done with Muhammad. If he could escape and build up a strong following in Yathrib, which was on their trade route, he would be a grave danger to them. On the other hand, to kill him would cause endless disputes with the clan of Hashim; and this would be an incalculable danger to Mecca and to the sanctity of the Ka'bah. After careful consideration, however, the meeting agreed with the proposal put forward by Abu Jahl, namely that each clan in Mecca should provide a young, powerful warrior, and that all these warriors should lie in ambush for Muhammad, and attack him together at once with sharp swords. In this way, they thought, they would be relieved of Muhammad while the responsibility for shedding his blood would be divided among all the tribes. The clan of Hashim would not then be able to fight against all the Arabs, and would have to accept Muhammad's murder as a *fait accompli*.

On the night they intended to murder him, Muhammad had planned to leave. Apart from a few who could not emigrate, chiefly for physical reasons, all his followers had already left Mecca safely, though they had left behind their properties and relatives. Only Abu Bakr and 'Ali were advised to postpone their departure. 'Ali was asked

*The Mosque at Quba'*

to sleep on Muhammad's bed and to cover himself with the Prophet's mantle. The idea was to make the party of youths waiting at the door of Muhammad's house, think that he was in his bed for the night, so that his departure might not be discovered until he had gone to a hiding place. The plan was successful.

Muhammad escaped from his house at night safely, and then joined Abu Bakr who had prepared two camels for the journey to Yathrib and hired a guide to lead them. Having left Abu Bakr's house by a back door, the Prophet and his companion proceeded southwards, in the opposite direction to Yathrib, in order to further mislead those who might pursue. When they reached the cave of *Thawr*, they concealed themselves in it for three days until the search for them by Quraish had relaxed. During these three days, Abdullah, son of Abu Bakr, called at the cave in the evenings and conveyed to them the news about Quraish who had offered a reward of one hundred camels for anyone who could bring Muhammad back. The shepherd of Abu Bakr's sheep also called in the evening, milked the sheep and gave Muhammad and Abu Bakr milk to drink, and then drove them back to Mecca covering on his way the tracks of Abu Bakr's son.

While they were hiding in the cave, a search party of the unbelievers reached the cave; but somehow it did not occur to them to look inside. They were deceived by the condition of the entrance of the cave which gave no indication of a recent penetration. When Abu Bakr saw their feet, he became worried and said, 'If any of them looks up from where he stands, we shall be discovered.' The Prophet replied, 'They are so many; but what do you think of two with Allah on their side?'[1]

After the period of hiding, Muhammad and Abu Bakr emerged from the cave. Accompanied by their guide and one of Abu Bakr's slaves, they went on their way to Yathrib, following devious tracks. It took them seven days to reach *Quba'* on the outskirts of Yathrib, where they stayed for four days and where Muhammad established his first mosque. On arrival at Quba', the danger was over.

Muslims in Yathrib, who by then were numerous, and who loved Muhammad exceedingly, had gathered every day at the way of approach from Mecca, eager to see their Prophet arriving in their town. Many of them were to see him for the first time.

On 24 September 622, 12 Rabi' al-Awwal, of the first year of the Islamic Era, Muhammad was seen coming with his party. The Yathribites accorded him a most enthusiastic welcome, chanting, together with their women and children, songs in his praise. Everyone wanted to be his host, but on his request the she-camel he was riding was left alone until she knelt down in the court-yard of the house of Abu Ayyub, Khalid Ibn Zaid. There the Prophet stayed till he purchased a plot of land, where he built his mosque in Yathrib with two rooms beside it for his residence. His wife, Sawdah, occupied one of the two rooms; and when he married 'A'ishah, she occupied the other room.

The mosque of the Prophet was built of simple material, and its roof, which was made of leaves and stalks of date-palms, was just above the height of an ordinary man. The mosque served as a place of public gathering, a place of devotion and prayer, and as a school where the Companions received guidance and instruction in their religion from their inspired leader.

Soon after, the Prophet replaced the name *Yathrib* by that of *Madinah*. By changing the denomination of the town, perhaps he intended to obliterate the memories of the heathen era. The journey from Mecca to Madinah became known as the *Hijrah,* and the lunar year in which it occurred was later chosen by the second Caliph, 'Umar, as the first year in the Islamic Calendar.

On arriving at Yathrib, Muhammad immediately set about his task. He did not allow the triumph of his escape from the Meccan persecution in reaching the safety of Madinah, or the enthusiasm and hospitality accorded to him by his followers, to blind him to the great difficulties he had to face in Madinah. In Mecca, although he was a spritual guide to his followers, and was concerned over their prosperity and well-being, Muhammad nevertheless was just an ordinary citizen, holding no authority and shouldering no formal responsibility. On reaching Madinah, he became the leader of a large community who looked upon him, not only as their deliverer, but also as their guide both in material and spiritual affairs. In other words, he became their ruler, responsible for law and order amongst them, and for their safety and protection against all dangers.

The Meccans, all of whose plans to kill or to capture Muhammad had failed, would not let him live in peace in

Madinah where he would be a constant threat to their caravans to Syria. Sooner or later, Muhammad was sure the Meccans would attack him and his town, and he had to guard himself against the possibility of being taken by surprise.

The internal situation of Madinah, moreover, was not quite safe. The Jewish tribes and their intrigues constituted a constant danger. They could conspire with the Meccans and spy for them. They could also create disruption among the Muslims themselves by reviving the bitter memories of the past.

Among the Muslim community, factors of disunity were very evident. The Muhajirun were northern Arabs, whereas the Ansar were southern Arabs; and the revival of ancient tension between the southern and northern Arabians would estrange the two groups from each other. Even within the group of the Ansar, the danger of disunity between the two major tribes of Khazraj and Aws was very real, as a result of the protracted feuds in the past and the intrigues of the Jews in former days.

The way in which Muhammad dealt with these problems reveals a high order of wisdom and ability, and his success in overcoming them was exceedingly great. His attitude towards these difficulties and how he tackled them gained him praise and admiration from all quarters for his skill and statesmanship.[2]

The Prophet averted the danger of the Jews, at least for the time being, by concluding with them a treaty of mutual respect and freedom of worship. He also successfully achieved a full social integration among his followers by denouncing all old tribal loyalties, and replacing them by the ties of Islamic brotherhood. To put this into practice, he united as full brothers every two Muslims, for example, one from the Muhajirun with another from the Ansar. This tie meant real mutual rights and obligations between the newly united brethren, including the rights of inheritance of property.

In this way, the Prophet created the concept of one *ummah* or one nation, united on the basis of a common belief and not divided on the basis of heterogeneous allegiances. The ancient loyalties and old disputes were forgotten, and all these were condemned as *Fahili*, that is, belonging to the age of ignorance and insolence. Moreover, the immense influence of the personality of the Prophet was another unifying factor. The model of the Prophet and the descent of the Qur'an for guidance under their eyes, reacted on the character of his Companions, and made every one of them an example of the Islamic virtues and ideals. Conversion to Islam cancelled the effect of all evil acts committed in the past by a convert; and a short stay in the company of the Prophet was believed to be enough for completely purifying a person and raising him to the highest ranks. Those Companions of the Arabian desert, made amazing achievements when they became later the masters of the world. No wonder; they had graduated in the school of the Prophet Muhammad.

---

[1] *Qur'ān, Chapter IX, v.* 40; *Matn al-Bukhari, Vol. II, p.* 288.
[2] *Encyclopaedia of Islam, s.v. Muhammad.*
[3] *Qur'an, Chapter XIII, v.* 38, *which reads: Say to the unbelievers, if they cease their insolence and rejection of the faith, the past will be absolved for them.*

NINE

# Reforms and Consolidation

Muhammad spent the first year of his stay in Madinah consolidating his position, inspiring his followers with the Islamic ideals and promoting strong ties of Islamic brotherhood between them. The practice of the five daily prayers which were performed regularly and collectively in the Prophet's mosque after ablution, and led by him, inspired the Muslim community of Madinah with the virtues of unity, discipline, orderliness, obedience, forbearance, mutual love, punctuality and cleanliness. The ritual of *adhan*, the call to prayer, chanted from the top of the mosque in the melodious voices of such people as Bilal Ibn Rabah, captivated their ears and softened their hearts.

The Prophet on reaching Madinah, held his first Friday congregation, and this henceforth became a weekly event. The sermon which was said before the Friday prayers offered an excellent opportunity for delivering concentrated teaching and guidance.

In the second year of the Hijrah the obligations of fasting in the month of Ramadan and of almsgiving were instituted; and in the course of time periodical congregations similar to those of Friday were established.

The frequent contacts between the individual and his Lord in prayers, and the practice of fasting, where all pleasures were given up voluntarily during the daytime for a whole month, were an effective training, which refined the earlier crude Bedouin character of the Companions of the Prophet, converted them into fine personalities, possessing integrity and wisdom, statesmanship and judgement, and gave them depth of knowledge and conscience. All these qualities enabled them to lead and rule successfully the extensive Muslim empire which was to grow up very soon. They could also effectively tackle the complicated and very thorny problems which were to face them, when multitudes of people, who formerly belonged to a variety of cultures and philosophies, came under the yoke of the Muslim State.

The obligation of alms-giving was a practical application of the principles of sacrifice, co-operation, and collective responsibility which emphasized the unity between the Muslims, and which took the wealth from the hands of the rich for the needs of the poor.

In the fifth year of the Hijrah, the obligation of pilgrimage to Mecca once in the lifetime of a Muslim was established, thus completing what have become known as the five pillars of Islam which are: the confession of the creed, the five daily prayers, fasting, almsgiving and pilgrimage.

Revelation continued to reach the Prophet on all sorts of occasions giving guidance and explanations to all questions, and instituting legislation in all aspects of life. Drinking wine and taking interest on loans were forbidden, and the prohibition of indecency and all immoral acts was reiterated. Specific punishments or indemnities for the commission of theft, highway robbery, adultery, false accusation of innocent people, and manslaughter were established. In the case of other offences, assessment was left to the discretion of the ruling power. On the other hand, legislation was established giving fairly detailed guidance in the matter of inheritance and in matters of marriage, including what should be observed in betrothal, the degrees of prohibition and the performance of marriage contracts. Teaching also included the essential marriage gift to be given by the bridegroom as a gesture to the would-be wife, mutual rights

*Pilgrims*

and obligations between the spouses and what should be observed in case of unavoidable separation.

Injunctions were also given on the subject of commercial activities in all their aspects, including the records of agreements between the parties and the way in which the records should be written. Moreover, teaching was given in the observation of the virtues of kindness and obedience to parents, helpfulness to relatives and neighbours, kindness to orphans and the poor, and help to slaves towards emancipation; and righteousness and good manners in general.[1]

The moral guidance of the Prophet at this stage reiterates the importance of the virtues of honesty, modesty, conscientiousness, co-operation, propriety, contentedness, keeping trusts and regard for the rights and feelings of others. It condemns cheating, falsehood, rancour, haughtiness, ostentation, hypocritical flattering, sneering at others, spying on them, back-biting and corruption of any sort. Working for a livelihood is highly praised; likewise discipline and obedience to authorities. Justice is central in the teaching of Islam. It is to be observed not only by rulers towards their subjects, but also in all kinds of dealings. Even a father is forbidden to favour his own child unless he extends similar favours to his other children. To be charitable to the weak and the needy, and to utter cheerful greeting to those who come your way, including children, are highly recommended virtues. A Muslim is defined as one from whom no harm reaches others. All believers are declared to be like the constituent bricks of a building, being indispensable for the strength of the whole structure. In a company of three persons, two are forbidden to whisper to each other. This, the Prophet says, hurts the feeling of the third. One should not cook food in the vicinity of his neighbour without sharing it with him, and the joy and happiness of his own children should remind him of those of his neighbour. Manners for eating and drinking also fall within the teachings of the Prophet. One should eat only when one feels hungry; two dates should not be eaten at a time; and a stomach should not be filled. Washing the hands is recommended both before and after food, and frequent brushing of the teeth is highly recommended. Spitting and easing one's self by the thoroughfare or near public places are frowned at. Blowing onto food, breathing in drinks and drinking from the mouth of a water-skin are discouraged.[2]

While the Prophet was training his followers in the humane teachings of Islam, he was always fully aware of the great dangers which surrounded him. His first duty, on the other hand, was to expand the circle of Islam through persuasion. From the beginning, he declared that his mission was for all mankind. He wanted therefore the voice of Islam to reach the ears of all those living on the globe. The powerful tribes of Mecca and their allies were actively suppressing Muhammad's peaceful activities. The uncouth Bedouin tribes round Madinah who looked upon raiding others and taking away their property as a virtue, were an immediate danger to the peace of Madinah. Quraish of Mecca and their agents were dangerously active among these crude tribes, inciting them against Muhammad. Further away, there were the great Powers of Byzantium and Persia who had each established a buffer Arab kingdom, as a satellite, to protect their boundaries adjacent to the borders of Arabia.[3] These two empires had feared the danger of the savage Bedouin Arabs when the latter were completely disunited.

In his town the Prophet was aware of the immediate danger from the Jews. They had hoped, it appears, that they could use him in their enmity against the Christians; but they found him sticking to his original teaching and exposing the errors and corruptions introduced by them in their original Gospel. Moreover, some of their leaders had embraced Islam, much to their surprise. They soon realized that they were continuously losing ground. They therefore started arguments merely designed to confuse the Divine guidance of Islam, and the dispute assumed a sharp character when the Ka'bah was made the *qiblah*[4] for the Muslim prayers instead of Jerusalem.

Not without Jewish influence, another dangerous group developed in Madinah headed by 'Abdullah Ibn Ubayy Ibn Salul, an ally of the Jews, who had been nearly elected head of Yathrib,[5] but the chance of this leadership was lost by the appearance of the Prophet on the scene. This group included all those with unfulfilled ambitions as a result of the flourishing of Islam in Madinah. They declared their conversion to Islam, but in fact they concealed their hatred to the faith and its Prophet. This group was called *al-Munafiqun,* the Hypocrites. As they were apparently Muslims, they had access to all information about the Prophet; and through them this was available to their secret allies.

Muhammad had to move very cautiously within these close and dangerous circles. He postponed sending messages of invitation to embrace the new faith to rulers abroad, until he had a fairly firm footing in Arabia. Muhammad rightly estimated the possible unfriendly reaction, if invitations to embrace the new faith were sent at that juncture to the rulers abroad. These foreign powers would no doubt fear the unity of the virile Arabs under the banner of the new faith; and to have had a direct contact with these rulers at this stage might have provoked them to crush the new religion in its infancy.

As for the Hypocrites, he accepted their superficial confession of faith, although there were clear signs of their insincerity. He adopted the principle of basing judgement on external submission and leaving to God what is hidden in the hearts of men. Even confession of the faith in suspicious circumstances had to be accepted. The Prophet bitterly blamed Usamah, son of Zaid, for having killed, in the heat of battle, an enemy who at the last moment shouted that there was no god but Allah. When Usamah claimed that the person did so only to save his neck, the Prophet retorted, 'Did you split open his heart?'[6]

Muhammad was not merely concerned about his own safety and the safety of his small group in Madinah, but also with the principles to be followed by the generations to come and by the Muslim world at large. Had he rejected the Hypocrites, he would have established suspicion as a principle of judgement, thus opening the gate to future despots who would liquidate their adversaries on suspicion or accusations, claiming to be following the example of the Prophet. It was better therefore to accept the Hypocrites in the ranks of Muslims; and to leave their intrigues to be skilfully dealt with by his superior ability. However, this group was bound to disband as a result of the growth of the strength of Islam and the gradual disappearance, by repentance or by death, of their insincere leaders.

Most of the Hypocrites were deeply touched by the attitude of the Prophet on the death of their paramount leader, 'Abdullah Ibn Ubayy in the ninth year of the Hijrah. In spite of all the serious troubles 'Abdullah had created for Muhammad at critical moments, the Prophet led the prayers over him, attended to all his funeral rites and was beside the grave during his burial. Many of the Hypocrites then repented and reformed themselves, and the backbone of this dangerous group was thus peacefully broken.

As for the Jews, the Prophet dealt with them as the occasion demanded. He combatted their arguments by argument, and he had the better of them. When they revived the pre-Islamic enmities between the groups within the Islamic community, the immense influence of the Prophet's personality could easily settle all arising disputes in the most amicable manner. But when they intrigued with the aggressive contingents which attacked Madinah, thus violating, at most critical moments, all solemn agreements they had earlier concluded with the Prophet, they were either exiled from the town or liquidated, not as in retaliation for their treacheries, but as a necessary measure of safety.

By the end of the fifth year of the Hijrah the Jewish danger was eliminated from the town of Madinah and all its outskirts. In just about a year from then, moreover, all the Jewish groups, scattered in the oases in Northern

Arabia were reduced, and they agreed to pay poll tax to the state of Islam in lieu of alms incumbent only on Muslims.

---

[1] *All these topics are dealt with mainly in the Qur'ān Chapters II, III and IV, three Madinan Chapters, augmented by the practice and injunctions of the Prophet.*
[2] *See various chapters on these topics in the major cannonical collections of Hadith.*
[3] *Supra, p. 5.*
[4] *Qiblah is the direction of the Ka'bah in Mecca which has to be faced during formal prayers.*
[5] *Supra, p. 46.*
[6] *Abu Zakariyya al-Nawawi, Riyad al-Sālihīn, Cairo, n.d., p. 77.*

# TEN

# Hostile Relations with Mecca

While Muhammad was tackling the problems of the Jews and the Hypocrites in Madinah, he was also taking precautionary measures against the danger of Quraish of Mecca. He could not reasonably remain passive in the face of their hostilities and their determination to annihilate him, waiting for them to surprise him in his retreat and crush him and his group. He had to be prepared for defence; but he did not take the initiative and never intended to provoke hostilities. Permission was given to him to fight those who fought him. The Qur'an declares, *'Those who are being attacked are given permission to fight back since they are wronged.'* And the Muslims were commanded, *'And fight in the cause of Allah those who fight you, and do not transgress, because God does not love those who transgress.'*

In the early days of Madinah following the Hijrah we hear of certain raids made by the Muslims on the Meccan caravans on their way to, or back from, Syria. Madinah dominated the trade route between Mecca and Syria, and this strategic location placed the Meccan caravans in an unfavourable position. Some of these raids were headed by the Prophet himself.

We also hear of certain expeditions consisting of small numbers of Companions going in the direction of Mecca. Some of these expeditions were sent with secret sealed instructions from the Prophet to be opened at certain points on their journey. This was of course a measure of precaution to maintain the secrecy of the destinations of the expeditions, bearing in mind that there were Hypocrites in the ranks of the Muslims who made a common cause with Muhammad's enemies both within and without. These raids and expeditions soon developed into a series of major battles, which ended in complete submission to Islam by all the people of Arabia.

One of these renowned early expeditions was that sent in Rajab, the sixth month of the second year of the Hijrah, headed by 'Abdullah Ibn Jahsh. It consisted of eight men including the leader, none of whom knew their real destination. They were given a sealed letter by the Prophet and instructed not to open it until they had covered a two-day journey from Madinah. When the letter was opened, it read, 'If you read this letter of mine, proceed until you arrive at Nakhlah. Then lie in wait for Quraish and bring us news of them.'[3]

The expedition travelled towards their destination, Nakhlah, which was between Ta'if and Mecca; but two of its members were lost on the way. The camel these two were riding in turn was lost; and while they were searching for the camel, they were spotted and taken prisoners by the Meccans. The rest of the group managed to reach Nakhlah, but they were also discovered by a passing caravan. Fighting took place. Although they were outnumbered, the Muslims killed one unbeliever, took two as prisoners, and the rest of the party which accompanied the caravan fled. The two prisoners and the spoils of the caravan were carried to Madinah.

This was the first fight that ever occurred in Islam; and that booty was the first ever gained by Muslims. As it is clear, this fighting was not invited or provoked by Muslims who went out simply on a reconnoitring expedition.

Biographers of the Prophet have misinterpreted these expeditions and raids as an intention of punishment or retaliation by the Prophet on the people of Mecca who had persecuted the believers, forced them to emigrate from their town, and taken over possession of their properties. Some non-Muslim authors have taken up this theory and exaggerated it. They have not only branded Muhammad as an aggressor, but have also claimed that he imposed his faith at the point of the sword.[4]

We emphatically disassociate ourselves from all these claims. The biographies of the Prophet were written long after his death, and they were written at a time when Islam reigned supreme and the Muslims were elated by their astonishing military successes. They were so obsessed by these victories that some of the early biographers of the Prophet gave their works the title *al-Maghazi,—the Battles*, thus unduly emphasizing the military aspect of the life of the Prophet. We can reject theories formulated by Muslim authors in this mood, which did not take a full account of the circumstances in which these events occurred.

On the other hand, we cannot agree with the claims of the orientalists. The first generation of this group of scholars did not apparently write on Islam merely from an academic angle. They had obviously politico-religious motives, and were biased and unjustifiably aggressive in their remarks and criticism of the Prophet. Muslims should guard themselves against such remarks creeping into the literature dealing with the Prophet and Islam. We do not, however, underrate the role played by the orientalists in the revival of the early Islamic literature through their unrelenting patience and labour. Nor do we underestimate the contribution made by the later generations of orientalists, who gradually freed themselves from the shackles of their masters, offering fresh theories and more enlightened interpretations in a more unprejudiced spirit.

We cannot agree, however, that the early expeditions sent by Muhammad towards Mecca or the raids conducted against its caravans were intended to impose Islam, or even meant to punish or provoke the Meccans, as enunciated by the early biographers and exaggerated by the later scholars. Such an attitude not only conflicts with the Qur'anic teaching against provoking aggression[5], but would also have been a most unwise course of action on the part of the man whose wisdom and fore-sightedness have been recognized by all. Muhammad's position in the early years of Madinah was vulnerable and precarious. To provoke at this juncture the powerful tribes of Mecca, with numerous allies throughout Arabia and particularly in the neighbourhood of Madinah, would have been fatal and suicidal. Moreover, the number of people in those expeditions was very small. The one sent to Nakhlah at the other side of Mecca, cited above, was made up of only eight men. It does not seem legitimate therefore to infer that Muhammad had intended to send these small missions to fight or provoke his powerful and numerous enemies.

Muhammad must have feared a surprise attack by the Meccans, and he had to send out these small groups of his Companions as reconnaissance missions in the direction of Mecca, to bring him information about the possible movements or concentrations of his enemies. That obviously justifies the smallness of the size of these expeditions, and this interpretation can be supported by the text of the sealed letter given to 'Abdullah Ibn Jahsh when he was sent out to Nakhlah. In that letter the expedition was instructed to observe from a hiding place the movements of Quraish and to report to the Prophet.

The activities conducted by the Muslims against the Meccan caravans, moreover, were not at all of the nature of the traditional raids of Arabia nor had they the same motives. The enemy caravans provoked and bribed the Bedouin tribes near Madinah, and the Prophet was fully justified in going out to curtail the hostile activities of these caravans and to deter the puppet Bedouins from aggression. This perhaps accounts for the reports that in nearly all cases the caravans escaped safely, which strengthens our conviction that Muhammad's intention in those ventures was neither to plunder the caravans nor to provoke fighting. His strategic position would have made it easy for him to lay ambushes on all the tracks, if this had been his intention. But as far as we can see these early activities were intended as a kind of psychological warfare of a deterrent nature. In most of these adventures, the Prophet concluded agreements of non-aggression or of mutual help with some of the neighbouring Bedouin tribes before he returned to Madinah.

The early Muslim expeditions consisted entirely or mainly of the Emigrants and not of the people of Madinah. This was not due to reluctance on the part of the latter to help the Prophet or defend him outside their town. The Emigrants belonged to a commercial community of habitual travellers, whereas the Ansar or Supporters of Madinah were mainly agricultural and a sedentary type of people. Therefore the Emigrants were more conversant with the tracks and paths between Mecca and Madinah, and being Quraishites themselves, they could discern the tricks of the Meccans. Moreover, the Supporters were the breadwinners, and the Emigrants were still mainly their guests. It was therefore befitting that the Emigrants should go out, while the Supporters were left at home.

The claim that Muhammad resorted to the sword to impose his religion is absolutely unjustifiable. It not only conflicts with the declared principle of the Qur'an which reads, '*There is no compulsion in religion*,'[6] but it also contradicts the nature of the faith itself. Faith is an internal mental process. It is a conviction which results from submission to certain premises in a logical manner. Therefore, it cannot be imposed by an outside agent through physical intimidation. You can perhaps impose an artificial outward obedience by physical means; but you cannot achieve a willing internal submission.

In addition to this logical argument, a careful analysis of the military events and the way in which they evolved would easily reveal that Muhammad, like most of the Muslim generations that followed, was always the victim of aggression. As we shall see, most of the battles took place in the neighbourhood of Madinah, and this is conclusive evidence that the aggressors travelled to attack him in his own town. His role was merely the defence of his faith and of his followers; and in the end he emerged from all the hostilities not only victorious but also the adored leader of his former enemies.

---

[1] *Chapter XXII, v.* 40.
[2] *Chapter II, v.* 186.
[3] *al-Sīrāh al-Nabawiyyah, pt. I, p.* 602.
[4] *Emile Dermenghem, The Life of Mahomet, pp.* 170 ff; *Karl Brockelmann, History of the Muslim Peoples,* London, 1952 *p.* 23; *B. Lewis, The Arabs in History, p.* 44.
[5] *Qur'ān, e.g., Chapter II, v.* 190, reads: *And fight in the way of Allah those who fight you, and do not start hostilities. Indeed God does not love the agressors.*
[6] *Chapter II, v.* 256.

# ELEVEN

# Major Military Engagements

The first major military engagement between Muhammad and the people of Mecca occurred in Ramadan of the second year of the Hijrah, March 624 A.D., just six weeks after the engagement at Nakhlah. It took place near a spring called *Badr*, nearly midway between Mecca and Madinah. The event was therefore called the Great Battle of Badr.

The Prophet had gone out at the head of 313 of his men (including about 86 Emigrants) to counteract the activities of a mighty Meccan caravan headed by Abu Sufyan, a shrewd grandson of Umayyah. There was no encounter between the Muslims and the caravan which proceeded safely to Mecca. Before Muhammad could return to Madinah he heard that Mecca had organized a powerful army made up of 950 men, including all the great warriors of Mecca, under the leadership of Abu Jahl, and that they were marching towards Madinah. Muhammad decided to intercept them, and instead of returning to Madinah, he marched towards Mecca until he met his enemies at Badr.

The Muslim force was not by any means a match for the Meccan army. Their number was very much less, and they were much inferior in weapons. After all, they had not expected to have such an encounter when they left Madinah. Yet, owing to their high spirits and to the distinguished leadership of Muhammad, the Muslims inflicted an amazing defeat upon their enemies. Most of the leading personalities of Mecca including Abu Jahl himself were amongst the seventy Meccan casualties; and when the unbelievers resorted to flight they left behind seventy prisoners and much booty to be carried away to Madinah.

This astonishing victory enormously enhanced the prestige of Muhammad throughout the Arabian world. From now on he was no longer a fugitive, but a real force to be seriously considered. Muhammad humbly returned to Madinah, full of gratitude and thanks to his Lord who had helped him and his men in their difficult circumstances. The spoils of war were distributed in a fair manner among the warriors; and those to whom the Prophet had assigned other duties at the time of fighting were not left out. Those who fought on foot were given one share each, and the few riders, knights, were given two shares each.

The Prophet then consulted his Companions over what should be done with the prisoners of war, having earlier forbidden any harsh treatment of them. There was a feeling among the Muslims, especially the Emigrants, that in view of these prisoners' evil deeds in the past, they should all be killed. But Abu Bakr intervened and said, 'O Messenger of Allah! They are your own people and your own relatives, and Allah has granted you victory over them. If you spare their lives, their ransom will be a strength to us, and God may guide them in the right path in which case they will be a support to you.'[1]

The Prophet agreed to spare the lives of the prisoners, as counselled by Abu Bakr. A ransom, however, was imposed upon those who could afford to pay it as a price for their release; but of those who knew the art of writing, each was to teach it to ten Muslim youngsters instead of paying a material ransom. The poor among the prisoners, however, were freed gratuitously.

Among the prisoners was al-'Abbas Ibn 'Abd al-Muttallib, a paternal uncle of the Prophet, who appealed for his freedom on the grounds that he had joined the Meccan army under pressure. Muhammad, nevertheless, refused to have him released until his ransom was paid.

The Prophet happened to see in the ransom paid on behalf of his son-in-law, Abu al-'As Ibn al-Rabi', the necklace of Zainab, his own daughter, which had been given to her earlier by her mother, Khadijah, at the time of Zainab's wedding. The sight of the necklace evoked the memory of Khadijah in the heart of the Prophet who suggested to his followers in a moving voice, "If you wish, you may return it to her.'[2]

The humane treatment of Muhammad towards his captives won him the hearts of many of his enemies. One of those freed, al-Walid Ibn al-Walid, was much influenced by what he had seen during his captivity. He was ransomed by his brothers, Khalid and Hisham, but on his return to Mecca, he declared his conversion to Islam. When his brothers blamed him for not having done this before, in order to save the ransom, he replied that he did not want to be accused of having been converted for a material motive. He had, however, to endure persecution for some years in Mecca before he could join the Prophet in Madinah.

The Muslims' decisive victory at *Badr* did not mean that things became subsequently easier for the Prophet. Abu Sufyan who succeeded Abu Jahl as leader of Mecca swore not to touch women or perfume until he had retaliated against Muhammad. Moreover, the humiliating defeat of Quraish aggravated the activities of their agents among the Jewish and Arab tribes round Madinah.

On the Prophet's return from Badr the Jewish tribe of Qainuqa' began to show malicious jealousy over his victory and started to indulge in intolerable and provocative activities. They behaved indecently against some Muslim women and began quarrels with the Ansar, which resulted in shedding some Muslim blood. Moreover, they repeatedly and openly threatened, 'Let Muhammad not be inflated by his victory at Badr. He will see his fate when he meets us in battle.'[4] The Prophet therefore had to lay siege to their quarters, and in two weeks time they agreed to go into exile.

Two months after the exile of Qainuqa', Abu Sufyan himself at the head of 200 men was active on the outskirts of Madinah trying to induce the other Jewish tribes to rise up in arms against Muhammad. He even burnt down some orchards and houses, and killed a Muslim; but when the Prophet went out to meet the aggressors on 5/12/2 A.H., they resorted to flight, dropping much of their provision of flour packed in large sacks, in order to make the flight lighter for their transport beasts. The flour was collected by Muslims, and the raid was therefore called Ghazwat al-Sawiq, the Battle of Flour.

Soon after the raid of Sawiq, some of the tribes of Ghatafan, an ally of Quraish, marched towards Madinah; but on 12/3/3 A.H. they dispersed when they heard that the Prophet was on his way to intercept them. Two months later the tribe of Sulaim attempted to do what the Ghatafan tribes had failed to achieve, but they also broke up and fled when the Prophet went out to meet them on 6/5/3 A.H.

Although Abu Sufyan believed that his vow was fulfilled by his recent misdeeds in Madinah on the day of Sawiq, yet he and Quraish were determined to inflict a larger punishment on the Muslims. All the proceeds of the Meccan caravan, which had escaped before Badr, were set aside for the cost of this adventure. In the eleventh month of the third year of the Hijrah, just one year after the battle at Badr, Abu Sufyan, at the head of 3,000 men, motivated by hatred and bent upon revenge, was approaching Madinah. Muhammad, under the pressure of the young Muslims who formed a majority in his consultative body, agreed to meet the aggressors outside, although he would have preferred to make his defence inside the town. When he was ready, the young men, who had realized their mistake in opposing the view of the Prophet, tendered their apology and offered to follow his original plan. The Prophet declared that he could not hesitate once he had decided on a course of action, thus giving his followers an excellent example both in real democracy and in determination.

Muḥammad met the enemy in the valley of one of the hills surrounding Madinah, called the Mount of Uhud. He had only seven hundred men. Thus the Muslim forces were apparently as much inferior in number as they were in arms; but they were strengthened by their faith and were guided by Muḥammad.

The Prophet nearly won this battle. But a mistake on the part of the Muslim archers, who acted against the Prophet's instructions, caused this engagement to end inconclusively with losses on both sides, but heavier this time for the Muslims. However, Madinah was saved; and Muḥammad pursued the enemy for miles on the way to Mecca.

Although the Meccans returned overawed by Muḥammad's determination, yet the misfortunes suffered on the Day of Uhud emboldened the Jewish tribes and the unruly Bedouins round Madinah against the Prophet. The three years which followed Uhud were a period of constant struggle. In the second month of the fourth year of the Hijrah, the Prophet suffered two treacherous blows at the hands of some Bedouins who called at Madinah deceitfully declaring their friendship and their conversion to Islam. The Prophet was persuaded by these callers to send away, in their company and under their protection, some of his Companions to guide them in the teaching of Islam. On the way to their respective destinations, the Companions were treacherously butchered. One of the groups consisted of ten Companions, and the other of seventy.

In the third month of the same year the Jewish tribe of Nadir nearly succeeded in their conspiracy to murder the Prophet himself. However, they were besieged, and like the tribe of Qainuqa', were forced to go into exile. In the third month of the following year Muḥammad had to go out with one thousand of his men to disband a concentration of Bedouins at *Dawmat al-Jandal* near the borders of Syria, who intended to march on his town. In the eighth month of the same year, the Prophet went out and defeated a large group of the tribe of *Mustaliq* who had conspired to destroy him. The enemy suffered heavy losses; and many of their men, women and children, together with large flocks of camels and sheep were captured by the Muslims.

It was in this expedition against the tribe of Mustaliq that the Hypocrites were permitted to join the Muslim army. The leader of the Hypocrites, 'Abdullah Ibn Ubayy Ibn Salul, however, created serious difficulties. He would have caused a sharp split within the Muslim forces had it not been for the great wisdom of Muḥammad. The gross crime of 'Abdullah provoked his own son to go up to the Prophet and seek his permission to behead his father. The Prophet rejected the request saying, 'Let not the people go round and claim that Muḥammad was killing his own followers.'[5]

When his design of splitting the Muslims failed, 'Abdullah and his agents went round with malicious rumours touching the honour of 'A'ishah, the young wife of Muhammad who accompanied him on this expedition. The fabricated scandal was a subtle design not only intended to reflect on the reputation of the household of the Prophet, but also to have far-reaching adverse consequences on the web of relations within the Muslim community. This gossip therefore created a considerable upheaval for some time in Madinah. Eventually a divine revelation asserted the fidelity of

'A'ishah and exposed her accusers.[6] It was a great relief to the innocent young lady and to the Muslim community at large; and a shame and humiliation to the Hypocrites.

---

[1] *Muḥammad Ibn Jarir al-Tabari, Jami' al-Bayan*, Cairo, 1954, Vol. X, pp. 41-2.
[2] *Alfred Guillaume, The Life of Muhammad*, Oxford University Press 1955, p. 314.
[3] *Abu 'Abd Allah al-Zubairi, Kitab Nasab Quraish*, Cairo, 1953, pp. 324 f.
[4] *al-Sirah al-Nabawiyyah*, pt. II, pp. 47 f.
[5] *Ibid*, p. 291 and p. 293.
[6] *Chapter XXII*, vv. 11-2.

# TWELVE

# Further Hostilities, and the Truce of Hudaibiyah

The eleventh month of the fourth year of the Hijrah witnessed the gravest threat to which Madinah and the religion of Islam were ever exposed. All the enemies of Islam at that time joined hands together for the purpose of completely destroying Muḥammad and his followers.

*Hayiyy Ibn Akhtab*, the leader of the Jewish tribe of *Nadir* which had been expelled from the town of Madinah a year previously, went to Mecca with a delegation from his tribe and invited Abū Sufyān, the leader of Quraish to join them in their efforts to eliminate Islam. In order to persuade the Meccans of his sincerity, Hayiyy and his fellow-men prostrated before the Meccan idols, which was an act contrary to the fundamental monotheistic principle of Judaism.

The allies of Quraish, the tribes of G̲hatafan and others, were brought into this Meccan-Jewish alliance. No less than ten thousand warriors under the leadership of Abu Sufyan, marched towards the town of the Prophet.

On hearing of this dangerous advance, the Prophet deliberated with his Companions who all agreed to remain in the town to defend it.

With the exception of its northern side, Madinah was naturally protected. On the advice of Salman, a Companion from Persia, a ditch was dug on the unprotected side to ward off the cavalry of the unbelievers. It was a novel idea, and the task of digging the ditch was a difficult one in which the Prophet took a full part.

The aggressors were surprised when they arrived and saw the ditch; they had to camp between the ditch and the road leading to the Mount of Uhud. Muḥammad, on the other hand, with all the forces available in Madinah, 3,000 in all, camped on the eastern side of the town, keeping guard on the ditch day and night.

Apart from some sporadic exchanges of arrows, some duels, and some unsuccessful attempts to cross the ditch by horsemen of the allied forces, there was no serious engagement between the two armies.

Nevertheless, the position of Muḥammad gradually deteriorated. Soon the Hypocrites became impatient and withdrew from the Muslim columns. This however was not such a serious setback, but when *Quraidhah*, the Jewish tribe whose dwellings and forts lay in the south of Madinah, secretly conspired with the aggressors, the situation became extremely critical.

Quraidhah, under the influence of the leader of the exiled Jewish tribe of Nadir, Hayiyy Ibn Akhtab, and in violation of the terms of their treaty with Muhammad, agreed that when the allies on a fixed day and time should make an all-out assault on Madinah from the north, Quraidhah would do likewise from the south, thus placing Madinah between the jaws of pincers.

The Prophet was not unduly perturbed, although by then only a few hundred of his men remained with him, pledging themselves to stand by him and to shed the last drop of their blood. On the one hand the Prophet lost no time in taking adequate measures to protect the lives of the Muslim families in Madinah. On the other, he successfully worked to outwit the stratagems of his enemies. During this dark moment, a man from the enemy camp crossed the ditch unseen, joined the Prophet and declared his conversion to Islam. Through this man, whose conversion was not known as yet to the unbelievers, the Prophet was able to disseminate discord and mutual mistrust between the leaders of the allies and those of Quraidhah. In the event co-operation between the conspiring parties became impossible, and their intrigues against Muhammad failed.

Seeing that the siege was becoming prolonged unfruitfully, the allies despaired and withdrew. Thus both the religion of Islam and Madinah were saved. Disgrace was the fate of the aggressors. As a consequence of the intrigues of Quraidhah during the siege, the following month saw their liquidation; so the town was finally cleared of the Jews.

The deliverance of Madinah from this dangerous siege was a great event, and the Prophet always remembered it with gratitude to God, 'Who alone defeated the allies.'[1]

The disappointment of the various groups which took part in this unsuccessful siege, however, enhanced their hatred and increased their belligerent activities against Muhammad. In the year which followed the siege, the sixth year of the Hijrah, the Prophet had to conduct no less than fifteen expeditions in various directions to disband aggressive concentrations against him. In addition an attempt on his life was unsuccessfully made by an agent of Abu Sufyan. None of these expeditions, however, involved a serious engagement; while the Prophet, towards the end of this year, secured a political success which had far-reaching consequences. In fact, it could be considered as one of the major diplomatic successes in the history of Islam.

The ritual of pilgrimage had been instituted during the previous year, and the Prophet had a dream which he wanted to fulfil. He dreamt that he was peacefully worshipping around the Ka'bah accompanied by his followers. Inspired by this dream, the Prophet decided to proceed towards Mecca at the head of 1,200 Muslims, who drove with them their sacrificial animals, already marked in order to display their peaceful intention.

The Muslims were, nevertheless, intercepted and prevented by Quraish from reaching Mecca. The Prophet had to camp with his men in a place called al-Hudaibiyah near Mecca. Messengers travelled between Quraish and Muhammad; and eventually a treaty was concluded with a ten-year truce between the two parties. During the period of this truce, the two parties undertook to respect pacts concluded by either side with a third party.

In order to secure this agreement, the Prophet yielded to two conditions laid down by Quraish, which were resented by the Companions of the Prophet, as they appeared to be humiliating to the Muslim party. Although these conditions aroused indignation among the Companions, yet because of the immense prestige of the Prophet they had to acquiesce.

The Prophet against the silent disapproval of his Companions, agreed to postpone his intention to perform the pilgrimage till the next year. Quraish insisted on this condition as a face-saving device for themselves. Muḥammad also undertook to return to Quraish anyone from Mecca who might escape to him without permission from his guardian; while Quraish were permitted to retain anyone who might join them from amongst Muḥammad's community.

Subsequent developments proved the far-sightedness of Muḥammad and showed that these conditions were in fact in his favour. On the one hand, it was far better and safer for the Muslims to pay their visit to Mecca and perform the Ka'bah rituals peacefully in the following year with the willing acceptance of Quraish who undertook to lay down their arms, and even to leave the town for the days assigned for the Muslims' visit. On the other hand, shortly after the conclusion of the treaty, Quraish themselves proposed the rescinding of the terms stipulating that any Meccan who became a Muslim and sought asylum in Madinah should be returned to Mecca. It happened that some Meccans, like al-Walid who was captured on the Day of Badr and subsequently released, turned Muslim and managed to run away to Madinah. The Prophet, much against his personal feelings, advised them to return to Mecca in fulfilment of the terms of the Treaty. They, however, did not go back to Mecca, but stationed themselves on the coastal trade route, dangerously threatening the safety of the Meccan caravans. The Prophet was happily prepared to oblige Quraish and welcome the Meccan fugitives in Madinah.

The advantages of this Treaty to Muḥammad cannot be over-estimated. On the one hand, it was a direct acknowledgement on the part of the Quraish that Muḥammad was their equal, a fact which they had so far obstinately refused to recognize. On the other hand, Muhammad very much needed a truce with Quraish. Such a truce would both have its pacifying effect on their allies and sympathisers, and would also enable him to attend to other pressing tasks. In fact, this was the first time that Quraish had ever agreed to leave Muḥammad in peace for a while, since he had proclaimed his message in Mecca nineteen years earlier.

The two years which followed the conclusion of the Truce, and which were relatively peaceful, witnessed events of great importance. On returning from Hudaibiyah, the Prophet without delay sent letters of invitation to the new faith to various leaders in all parts of Arabia and also to some rulers abroad. They included messages to the rulers and princes of Byzantium, Egypt, Damascus, Persia, Bahrein, Abyssinia, Yamamah, Busra and Oman. Most of these rulers sent friendly replies, and some of them returned

*Letter supposed to have been sent by the Prophet to al-Mundhir*

the Prophet's ambassadors with valuable gifts. A few of them embraced Islam. The Muslim immigrants in Abyssinia were pleased to see the messengers who carried the message of the Prophet to the Negus. When they heard of the Truce, they decided to join their brothers in Madinah. These invitations, also, were a practical hint that the scope of Islam was not circumscribed by the boundaries of Arabia.

Another salutary effect of the Truce was the conversion to Islam of some eminent leaders of Mecca. The absence of hostilities between Muḥammad and Quraish enabled them to assess Muḥammad's claims without prejudice. Those converted included such personalities as Khalid Ibn al-Walid and ʿAmr Ibn al-ʿAs, both of whom left Mecca and joined the Prophet in Madinah, thus adding both to the moral and material strength of Islam. A year after the conclusion of the Treaty of Hudaibiyah, the Prophet and his followers fulfilled their wish and peacefully performed the pilgrimage in Mecca.

The peace of this period was however broken by certain provocations. The Jews were forming armies and carrying out manoeuvres against Muhammad in the scattered oases in Northern Arabia. The messenger of the Prophet to the Prince of Busra in Syria was brutally murdered on the way. Such a humiliation if tolerated would lead to more serious violations. Also, the Romans[2] displayed symptoms of hostility towards Islam, apparently in their fear of the growing unity of the Arabs under the banner of the new faith.

In the first month of the seventh year of the Hijrah the concentration of Jews at Khaibar was completely destroyed, and their fate was decided. The Jews agreed to pay taxes to Madinah.

The Prophet, in the fifth month of the eighth year also sent an expedition made up of 3,000 Muslims to meet the transgressors on their own soil at *Mu'tah*. A huge Roman army exceedingly superior in arms and in number was waiting; and in the fierce fighting some eminent Companions were lost, including Zaid, Muḥammad's emancipated and faithful slave and his adopted son, and Ja'far Ibn Abu Talib, his cousin who had recently returned from Abyssinia. The bulk of the Muslim army was, however, saved by the military genius of Khalid Ibn al-Walid, whom the Prophet then called 'The Unsheathed Sword of God'. This battle was perhaps the first military conflict between the Roman forces and Islam.

In addition to these engagements with the Jews and the Romans, a few expeditions were sent out by the Prophet to quell some Bedouin uprisings, in all of which the Muslim Companions were victorious. All these achievements, however, were overshadowed by the peaceful and glorious conquest of Mecca in the ninth month of the eighth year of the Hijrah.

---

[1] *Matn al-Bukhārī, Vol. I, p.* 309.
[2] *In Islamic annals the Byzantines are usually referred to as Romans.*

# THIRTEEN

# Marriages of the Prophet

During the Prophet's short stay in Mecca in the seventh year of the Hijrah when he performed the ritual of pilgrimage in fulfilment of the terms of the Treaty of Hudaibiyah, he married his last wife, Maimunah bint (daughter of) al-Harith on the suggestion of his uncle al-'Abbas. Maimunah was a widow of Abu Ruhm, another uncle of Muḥammad who fell on the day of Uhud and whose body was severely mutilated by Hind, wife of Abu Sufyan, in revenge for her father and brother who were among the Quraish victims on the day of Badr.

The marriage to Maimunah brought the number of the Prophet's marriages to eleven; and since two former wives had died earlier, Maimunah was to join a household in which she would be the ninth wife. Her co-wives were Sawdah bint Zam'ah, 'A'ishah bint Abu Bakr, Hafsah bint 'Umar, Umm Salamah, Umm Habibah, Zainab bint Jahsh, Juwairiyah bint al-Harith and Safiyyah bint Huyayy Ibn al-Akhtab. The two wives who did not survive the Prophet were Khadijah bint Khuwailid and Zainab bint Khuzaimah.

To be the wife of the Prophet, for any woman at the time, was an unequalled honour and an unmatched privilege. Each of these illustrious ladies was given the venerable title of *Umm al-Mu'minin* which means Mother of the Faithful. With the exception of 'A'ishah, their nuptial tie with the Prophet was not their first experience of marriage; and with the exception of Khadijah none of them bore a child to the Prophet. Only the servant girl presented to him by the Governor of Egypt gave birth to a son, Ibrahim, towards the end of the Prophet's life, but Ibrahim did not survive his father.

The marriage reforms brought about by Islam restricted every man to a maximum of four wives; and in order to ensure justice in the fulfilment of the conjugal duties and rights, it appeared that a man should not marry more than one wife except where exceptional circumstances justified the need for more than one. In no circumstances, however, was a man permitted to exceed the number of four.[1]

The Prophet, however, maintained nine wives at a time, all of whom survived him. This has given rise in recent times to a severe attack on the Prophet by certain non-Muslim authors who claimed that Muḥammad allowed himself what he had forbidden to others and associated his polygamy with an increase in his sensual love for women in the latter part of his life.[2] They even accused him of having been a man of lust who did whatever he wanted in quest of the satisfaction of his sensual desires.

This is certainly a misguided view based on mistaken moral values. It is unsound to condemn a mode of behaviour pursued in Arabia more than thirteen centuries ago, on the basis of the European moral standard of today.

Muḥammad's marriages should not be considered in isolation. They can be understood and appreciated in relation to his status and in the light of the circumstances in which these marriages took place.

Let us first of all bear in mind that the restriction on the number of wives a man could marry was instituted in Islam in the eighth year of the Hijrah, about a year after the last marriage of the Prophet. Therefore the claim that Muḥammad permitted himself what was forbidden to his followers is easily dismissed. Moreover, we very well know that the Prophet married Khadijah, a widow about fifteen years his senior, when he was about twenty-five years old; and continued with her alone until she died when he was over fifty. In other words, during the prime of Muḥammad's life he did not marry more than one wife. This would not have been the case if his polygamy in later years when he became very heavily burdened with formidable tasks, had been due to excessive sexual inclination. Polygamy was an ordinary practice among the pre-Islamic and contemporary Arabs, and Muḥammad could have easily added more wives during the life of Khadijah had he been under the influence of sensual factors.

The Prophet's polygamy, moreover, started in Madinah. If it were in any way due to the alleged considerations or were it to reflect on his morality, he would not have been spared from the tongues of the Hypocrites. The fabricated scandal involving his wife, 'A'ishah, which was discussed earlier was an attempt to reflect on the Prophet's character and it shows the keenness of the Hypocrites to grasp any opportunity for creating scandal.

Muhammad, when he emigrated to Madinah, assumed and combined a number of offices. In addition to being a religious teacher, he became at the same time a legislator, a political leader and a general. In the light of the obligations arising from these offices and of the moral values and habits obtaining at the time, the plurality of his wives which started only when he assumed these offices can be understood.

Anthropologists in recent years have discovered the significance of the size of the number of a chief's wives, which does not necessarily tie up with the chief's sensual inclination. Muḥammad and his nascent religion ran through very delicate moments; and the ties forged by Muḥammad's marriages must have had their political significance. Marriage ties, we can see, were established between him and his closest friends. He was a son-in-law of Abu Bakr and 'Umar, and father-in-law to 'Uthman and 'Ali. Another example of the Prophet's marriages with a political significance occurred when the expedition of the Prophet broke up the concentrations of the tribe of al-Mustaliq. A large number of the men, women and children of the defeated enemy were taken as prisoners of war. The Muslims wished to keep the captives as slaves or concubines; but al-Mustaliq were a people of honour and prestige in Arabia. It happened that Juwairiyah, daughter of the chief of Mustaliq was among the prisoners. The Prophet emancipated and married her. The Muslims then felt that they should not keep in slavery or in concubinage those who had become the in-laws of the Prophet; and as a result of this marriage the prisoners were all freed.

Humane and religious considerations also played their part in the Prophet's marriages. Take for example his marriage to Zainab bint Khuzaimah whose physical features were described as not particularly attractive. Her husband was killed in the Battle of Badr which was the first military battle in Islam. The loss of life in this battle was severely felt; and the Prophet must have meant by this marriage to show that the dependants of those lost in the defence of Islam were not to be neglected. This also applies to the case of Umm Salamah, whose husband was killed in similar circumstances. She and her children fell under the care and protection of the Prophet on her marriage to him.

The suffering of Umm Habibah bint Abu Sufyan was also great. She, together with her Muslim husband, was amongst those who emigrated to Abyssinia. In that country she was separated from her husband who came under the influence of the local Christians. She was later carried to Madinah in distressing conditions. Her father Abu Sufyan was leading the aggressive camp of unbelievers against

Muḥammad whose faith she had embraced. There could be no better consolation to her than to become a Mother of the Faithful.

The marriage of Zainab bint Jahsh was of a different character. She was the daughter of the Prophet's paternal aunt; and the Prophet had known her well since her childhood. When she reached marriageable age, Zaid Ibn Harithah proposed to her. This Zaid had been a slave of Muḥammad whom he had freed and adopted as a son in the pre-Islamic fashion. He was therefore called Zaid Ibn or son of Muḥammad. Islam later cancelled this habit of adoption and established that everyone should be called after his real father.[3] Islam was concerned with the legitimacy of children and with the removal of confusion in the matter of descent, so that everyone would look after his own children in accordance with his natural feelings of affection. Zaid was thenceforth called after his own father.

Because Zaid was a freed man, Zainab, who was descended from the best line of Quraish, refused his hand. The Prophet intervened and condemned such pre-Islamic vanity Zainab then had to yield, but owing to her vanity and disrespect to her husband, the marriage was never a happy one. Eventually the marriage was broken.

The cancellation of the practice of adoption of other people's children and the prohibition of all that used to go with it, legislated against a deeply-rooted custom. It was very difficult and even unimaginable for an Arab to violate the ancient habit; and such a violation would appear to him as an incestuous act. It was only the Prophet who could first break away from this established pre-Islamic tradition.

An adopted son, according to pre-Islamic customs, would stand in the full position of a real son, and his wife was therefore considered a daughter-in-law. The adopting father could not marry her on her separation from his adopted son, as he could not marry a former wife of his real son. When Zainab was divorced from Zaid, Muḥammad married her in the Islamic tradition against the pre-Islamic custom, thus emphasizing the ineffectiveness of the ties created by adoption of children.

From the above explanation it appears that the plurality of the marriages of the Prophet was quite justifiable, and the motives were not over-sexuality or the pursuit of sensual satisfaction. It is also not legitimate to claim that the Prophet permitted himself what he forbade to others.

When the legislation forbidding the marriage of more than four wives was established about a year after the last marriage of the Prophet, it is true, Muslims at the time had to divorce those women who were in excess of the rule. Divorced wives of ordinary men were normally desirable to others and were likely to be re-married. But it would have been drastic if a woman, who had enjoyed the status of Mother of the Faithful, were to be divorced by the Prophet, as no one would have thought of marrying someone who used to belong to the Prophet. Moreover, apart from certain humane considerations, discrimination in the choice of those to be divorced and those to be retained by the Prophet would possibly have had its political implication. By exempting the Prophet from the limitation of this legislation, which was quite harmless and which was the only exemption the Prophet claimed, these difficulties and hardships were easily avoided.

As it happened this exemption was not without its blessing to Islam. Those degnified Mothers of the Faithful who survived the Prophet transmitted to the world of Islam abundant information about the practices of the Prophet at home, which they had watched intimately. Their information was an immense treasure for the guidance of Muslims.

An important feature of the domestic life of the Prophet was his justice and the complete equality with which he treated all his wives. The Prophet, in spite of his hard tasks and occupations, never failed in the fulfilment of their rights or in giving them due care and attention. This was not only in matters of maintenance and provision, but also in the equally important human relations. He used to spend one night with each one of his wives in turn, and, whenever he was to travel, he drew a lot to determine which one of them was to accompany him. When they happened to be together with him, each wife received an equal share of his smiles and affection.

The Prophet, to be sure, appears to have developed some special affection for some of his wives, but this did not cause him to favour them over the others. In fact he used to say, whenever he felt this unequal internal division, 'God forgive me. This is my division in what I possess and that is your division in what You possess.'[4]

In spite of his status and the supreme reverence in which he was held, the Prophet treated his wives with unmatched kindness and good nature. He used to play and joke with them, and did not deny them the right of relaxation and entertainment. He was so indulgent and patient with them that they used to answer him back and to argue with him. He did not even approve of the harsh intervention by some of his fathers-in-law on hearing of their own daughters' taking advantage of the Prophet's clemency.

No wonder then that it was Muḥammad who saved the fair sex from their previous plight, and in his new system he raised them to a degree of esteem which they had never previously attained. Complete equality between the sexes within the framework of biological divergence was fully recognized. To criticize Muḥammad's teaching on the grounds of permitting a circumscribed polygamy is to ignore the biological and psychological factors involved and to disregard certain important sociological needs. To argue adversely on moral grounds is a sheer misuse of the moral concepts, and is a deliberate disregard of the widespread violation of sexual morality where this circumscribed polygamy is proscribed. The severe seclusion of women in some parts of the Muslim world is more a social than a religious question; and the results of its development are to be sought in the social history of Islam. Islam merely teaches us to observe propriety, and wants the female to maintain her dignity and preserve her modesty. This no doubt adds to her charm and attraction.

[1] *Qur'ān, Chapter IV, vv.* 3 *and* 129.
[2] *E.g. Emile Demenghem, The Life of Mahomet, pp.* 269 *ff*
[3] *Quar'ān, Chapter XXXIII, vv.* 4 *and* 5.
[4] *Abū Dāwūd, Sunan, Cairo,* 1950, *Vol. II, p.* 326.

FOURTEEN

# Conquest of Mecca

In the Treaty of Hudaibiyah concluded between Muḥammad and Quraish of Mecca towards the end of the sixth year of the Hijrah, the two parties undertook to respect all pacts of mutual protection established by either side with a third party. It happened that there were two clans with ancient mutual feuds living in the neighbourhood of Mecca, called Bakr and Khuza'ah. The clan of Bakr entered into alliance with Quraish and the clan of Khuza'ah entered into alliance with the Prophet.

Muhammad was faithful to the terms of the Treaty; but Quraish soon afterwards revealed their unreliability. Before the passage of two years from the date of signing it, the Treaty was flagrantly violated by Quraish.

It happened that a member of the clan of Bakr provoked a member of the clan of Khuza'ah by reciting anti-Muḥammad poetry, which he himself had composed in abuse of the Prophet. A quarrel started between these two men, but the dispute could have been settled. Nevertheless the bitter memories of the past were revived in the minds of the clan of Bakr. With military assistance from their allies, Quraish, they treacherously attacked the quarters of Khuza'ah, Muḥammad's allies, and killed more than twenty members of the clan.

Soon after, Quraish realized the degree of danger their action had precipitated, and they began to deliberate over what they should do in order to mend the situation. Muḥammad, by virtue of their action, had been placed in a position in which he was compelled to take action against the aggressors.

Some Quraishites proposed complete abrogation of the Treaty with Muhammad, and a return to the pre-Hudaibiyah days. A more moderate attitude, however, prevailed; and in order to confuse the situation, Abu Sufyan was sent on a mission to Madinah to seek a reaffirmation of the Treaty and to have its term extended.

Abu Sufyan's mission, however, was unsuccessful; but he obtained a first-hand impression of the unrivalled adoration and reverence accorded to Muhammad by his followers in spite of his modesty. On his return to Mecca, Abu Sufyan was accused of having embraced the faith of Muḥammad, because of his favourable description of what he had seen in Madinah. In order to vindicate himself, however, Abu Sufyan prostrated in front of the idols of the Ka'bah.

The Prophet, on the other hand, received a delegation from his allies who came to appeal to him for help. He could not by any means fail them. Leading ten thousand Muslims, Muhammad in the middle of Ramadan of the eighth year of the Hijrah marched towards Mecca. In order to avoid a serious clash with Quraish in the sacred town of the Ka'bah, he concealed his destination from all except his closest Companions. The Prophet with his men continued their successful march, reassured by encouraging Qur'anic revelations, until they reached *Marr al-Dhahran* near Mecca, where they camped for the night. Quraish had got word of a big Muslim expedition, but was not sure of its destination.

Abu Sufyan, together with a few others, left Mecca to find out, and were impressed by what they saw. They went up to the Prophet of their own accord and declared their conversion. The Prophet was very pleased with this achievement.

In order to avoid shedding blood as far as possible, the Prophet sent an announcement to Quraish through Abu Sufyan, in which he declared an amnesty for all who would stay peacefully at home, to those who would seek refuge in the Sacred Mosque, and to those who would seek protection in the house of Abu Sufyan. This was a generous gesture to the man who until recently had been the leader of the Sacred Town.

In order to invade Mecca from all directions, Muḥammad divided his forces into four columns, but ordered that fighting should be avoided as far as possible. Only the wing led by Khalid Ibn al-Walid faced a little resistance on its march from the southern direction.

On Friday, twentieth Ramadan, Muhammad, amidst his men and on the back of his she-camel, with his head lowered in humility to Allah, entered the gates of Mecca, reciting prayers in praise of God and in gratitude to the Almighty. Still on the back of his camel, surrounded by his adoring followers and watched by the huge crowds of Quraish who sought refuge in the mosque, Muḥammad performed the circumambulation of the Ka'bah pointing to the idols and declaring. 'Truth has been fulfilled and falsehood has gone.'[1] On his orders, all the idols were immediately dashed to pieces.

The Prophet then turned to Quraish who were apprehensively waiting to hear the word from him which was to decide their fate. He cried, 'Quraish! How do you think I am going to deal with you?' They answered, 'We think well. You are a noble brother and the son of a noble brother.' The Prophet said, 'Go into freedom; you are liberated.' He then added, 'Quraish! God has taken away from you the vanity of the olden days and the pride in your descent.'[2] He also added certain pronouncements of a legal character.

Now all factors which had caused the Meccans to resist the Islamic faith so vehemently had gone. The Kingdom of Heathenism of which they were the custodians had been ruined. With it their prestige and economic superiority were brought to an end. The persecuted fugitives from Mecca had returned to it as its conquerors. Realizing all these facts, Quraish had no further reason to reject the faith of the rectitude of which they no doubt had always been aware. It was only their vanity and the preservation of their worldly privileges which had prevented them from acknowledging the truth. They therefore came forward in large numbers and declared their conversion to Islam. Those who had formerly been particularly harsh to the Prophet, or who had committed violent offences, came humbly and offered their apologies to him. They were all very touched by his modesty, kindness and forgiveness.

Thus the seat of Heathenism had capitulated to Islam. With it the military opposition to Muḥammad in Arabia came nearly to an end. The turn of Ta'if came soon. A huge army of the tribes of *Hawazin* and *Thaqif* in the neighbourhood of Mecca engaged the Prophet immediately after the Conquest, but was broken up on the Day of *Hunain* and a very large amount of property was seized as booty. From these spoils the Prophet paid generously to the new Meccan converts, thus helping them to overcome past feelings and prejudices.

After settling matters of administration and appointing a governor in Mecca, the Prophet together with his men proceeded happily and cheerfully back to Madinah, full of gratitude to Allah for His help and guidance. The Prophet lived there for another two years, a period which we may call The Post-Conquest Era. It was an era of real peace in Arabia which ushered in the age of which the Prophet had been assuring his Companions since the beginning of the persecution in Mecca in the following words, 'A time will come when everyone of you will be able to travel alone from Mecca to San'a (in the Yemen), fearing nothing but God and the wolf over his sheep.'[3]

The news of the Conquest of Mecca and the impending unification of Arabia must have reached the ears of the people outside the Peninsula. This significant development appears to have precipitated an unfriendly reaction on the part of Persia, Byzantium and the East African states, who apparently feared the growing strength of the virile Arabs. We have seen how this fear had provoked the Byzantines on the signing of the Hudaibiyah Truce to urge their satellite, the Ghassanid Kingdom in Syria, to adopt a hostile attitude against Islam; and as a result the Battle of Mu'tah which was described above took place. Now the conquest of Mecca invoked further hostilities on the part of these neighbouring countries. An expedition from the direction of Abyssinia sailed across the Red Sea, and landed on an island facing Jeddah, preparing for an assault on the western coast of Arabia. On hearing of this, the Prophet sent a contingent which overcame the aggressors who withdrew without any more ado.

A more serious danger was a Byzantine concentration in Syria which, as the Prophet heard, was preparing an all-out attack on Arabia. It was just before the harvest season of Madinah, and the treasury was nearly empty. As a result, of the Prophet's appeal, however, wealthy Muslim personalities came forward with large contributions towards the cost of the expedition to Syria to meet the enemy. In the seventh month of the ninth year of the Hijrah, the Prophet led out a big army consisting of 30,000 Muslims, and marched north towards Syria to meet his formidable enemy. But by the time the Muslim forces reached Tabuk, on the Syrian borders, the enemy had withdrawn.

Having overawed the major enemy, the Prophet decided to return to his capital after concluding agreements with certain princes in the area. These rulers in their respective treaties undertook to pay tribute to the capital of Islam. This, however, did not end the hostile relations with Syria and the neighbouring territories. Provocative acts on the part of his enemies continued, and the Prophet was determined not to give a chance to the great powers, especially Persia and Byzantium, to take advantage of the nascent Islamic nation. The Prophet, therefore, early in the following year, organized another army to march towards the north. He, however, did not live long enough to see this army depart from Madinah. It was left to his successors to deal with the provocations of the adjacent countries; and it was because of these provocations and the reactions of the Muslims to them that the empire of Islam emerged and expanded in an amazingly short span of time.

A biographer of the Prophet Muḥammad will always be aware of six important developments in the Prophet's career which were all turning points in his life. Firstly his marriage to Khadijah which released his intellectual powers and enabled him to devote more time to contemplation and religious thinking. Secondly the proclamation of his mission when he was forty, in the year 622 A.D., which ushered in an era of severe persecution and hardahip for himself and his adherents. Thirdly the Hijrah to Madinah which opened up new territories for the expansion of his new faith. Fourthly his decisive victory over Quraish on the Day of Badr which astounded all Arabia and immensely raised his status and enhanced the prestige of his community. Fifthly his great diplomatic success at Hudaibiyah which in fact prepared the way for the sixth and most glorious event crowning all his other successes, namely the Conquest of Mecca.

---

[1] *Qur'an, Chapter XVI, v.* 81; Mohammad Husain Haikal, *Hayat Muhammad,* p. 423.
[2] *al-Sirah al-Nebawiyyah, pt. II, p.* 412.
[3] *Matu al-Bukhārī, Vol. II, p.* 281 and 321.

# FIFTEEN

# The Last Two Years

The post-Meccan Conquest Era was a period of consolidation and construction. During this period the Prophet developed further the system of his teaching and laid down many of its principles. He also completed the expansion of the faith throughout Arabia by peaceful means, thus creating for the first time a unified Arabia. The model of the Islamic state which became the prototype of the forthcoming Islamic empire was established.

The ninth and tenth years of the Hijrah witnessed the arrival in Madinah of many delegations from distant Arab tribes who came to declare their conversion and to pledge their loyalty. They were cordially met by the Prophet, who instructed them in religious matters, and sent each of them back with a teacher to guide them, to settle their disputes, to lead them in their prayers, to teach them the Qur'an and to represent the Prophet amongst them.

These events were reported in detail with painstaking exactitude, and these reports became an immense source for Islamic legal and theological knowledge. On the other hand, the Prophet sent messengers to invite other distant communities to embrace the new faith, thus establishing for the generations to come, the example of peaceful missionary work. A famous mission was that led by 'Ali Ibn Abu Talib, sent to the tribe of *Madhhij* in the Yemen. 'Ali was instructed by the Prophet, 'Invite them to the confession of Islam. If they do, teach them how to say the five daily prayers; and do not demand of them any further. And do not fight them unless they fight you.'[2] All these peaceful missions were successful.

Through these missions and through the delegations which called on the Prophet in Madinah, allegiance to the authorities of the capital of Islam was pledged by all communities in all parts of Arabia. Thus, the tribal system in the Arab Peninsula was largely dissolved, and the whole Arabian world became united under the leadership of Muhammad. Within this union the Prophet laid down the foundations of the Islamic state. All the Arabs had become one large unit under a central authority with its headquarters at Madinah. He appointed viceroys and governors to rule the provinces and settle disputes justly on his behalf. He told them to follow the Qur'an, but if they did not find the solution for their questions therein they were ordered to follow his practice. If they still could not find the answer in either of these ways, they were permitted to use their own judgement.[3]

Muhammad and his teaching have become in recent years a target for the arrows of certain unfriendly non-Muslim writers. By virtue of their training and upbringing they cannot see Muhammad except through prejudiced minds, and can not assess his achievement with justice or detachment. Islam would not have survived if their criticisms had been valid.

These writers claim that some inconsistency exists in the Qur'an, especially in relation to passages concerned with the degree of the freedom of man to choose the course of his own action.[4] They further claim in this connection that Muhammad's teaching implies that God is capricious, and that He arbitrarily chooses whom ever he wishes for either salvation or damnation.[5] They go further and assert that this dogma of fatalism is responsible for the tardiness and degeneration prevailing in some parts of the Muslim world today.

Inconsistency in the Qur'an would not have escaped the attention of Muhammad's contemporary adversaries especially in Mecca. When the Qur'anic verse which reads, 'Indeed you and those you worship apart from Allah will be firewood in Hell'[6] was revealed, a storm started among Quraish who thought that this would be the end of Muhammad. They rushed up to him and argued, 'You have been praising Christ and claiming that he was one of the distinguished messengers of your God, and now you claim that anything which is worshipped, apart from Allah, will go to Hell, together with its worshippers!' The Prophet silenced their clamour by stating that those who wished to be worshipped would be in the Fire with those who worshipped them.

This shows that Muhammad's contemporary adversaries were alert to any weakness by which they could attack him. In the absence of records of any other accusation of inconsistency by the contemporary Arabs and the many generations which followed, who understood the Arabic idiom far better than those unfriendly writers who have their linguistic handicaps, we can easily conclude that the latter failed to understand or rather that they misunderstood the text.

The claim that Islam is fatalistic has no firm grounds. It arises from this linguistic misunderstanding and takes root from the mistaken attitude of resignation which prevails among some misguided Muslims. Islam inspired the individual with courage and respect and intensified the sense of responsibility in him. Efforts in worldly pursuits are highly praised, and idleness and languor are condemned.

Some of those foreign authors depict the obligation of *Jihad*, normally translated as 'holy war', in a picturesque manner and claim that Islam is belligerent and intolerant.[7] They also take stock of the principle of *Jizyah*, the poll tax imposed on non-Muslims in a Muslim state.

We have seen that all the military activities of the Prophet were in defence against aggression; and that the teaching of the Qur'an and the practice of the Prophet up to the end of his life were not to fight except after provocation or in defence. Therefore to claim that the spirit of Islam is belligerent has no foundation. Moreover, non-Muslim residents in a Muslim state were to pay the poll tax as a contribution to the maintenance of the state by its non-Muslim citizens, in return for their protection and the other services rendered by the State. Non-Muslim women, children and the old and also those who could not afford it were exempted from payment of this tax. Muslim citizens, on the other hand, were under the obligation to give alms to the state. All able-bodied Muslims were to render military service in the Muslim state. From these two obligations non-Muslim citizens were exempted. It was, therefore, fair that they should also make their contribution towards the services offered by the state in return for the benefits and the security they enjoyed.

After his return from the Conquest of Mecca, and apart from his journey to Tabuk, the Prophet did not leave Madinah except when he travelled to Mecca at the end of the tenth year of the Hijrah to lead the season of pilgrims in Mecca. The previous year he had appointed Abu Bakr to this post. This pilgrimage of the Prophet has become known as the Farewell Pilgrimage because it was his last pilgrimage. During this season the Prophet delivered the famous Farewell Speech which he made on the Mount of '*Arafat* where the pilgrims had gathered in tens of thousands. He began this speech as follows: 'People! Hearken to me. It may be I shall not see you after this year in this place.'[8] Then he reiterated the principles relating to the unity of God, the unity and equality of mankind, respect for the rights and property of others and the preservation of trusts. The Prophet also repeated the prohibition of the adoption of the children of others, of *riba* (interest on loans) and of certain other evil pre-Islamic practices. The Prophet was particularly emphatic on the subject of the mutual rights between men and women in his speech. In this connection he said, 'People! For your women

*The Mosque of Madinah*

there is a right over you, as there is a right for you over them. Women should not allow others to step into your sleeping quarters, or permit others into your houses without your permission. They should not commit indecency. If they do, God has permitted you to make it uneasy for them and to sleep away from them. You may even beat them but not severely or in a humiliating manner. If they repent and obey you it is incumbent on you to provide for them in the prevailing manner. Your women are trusts in your hands. They cannot help themselves much. You marry them with a pledge to Allah, and they are permissible to you (in marriage) by the word of Allah. Fear Allah in the matter of women, and exert yourselves to do good and kindness to them.'[9]

Shortly after the Prophet's return from this pilgrimage he fell ill, and Abut Bakr was appointed to succeed him in leading the prayers in the mosque.

Muslims became worried over the illness of their Prophet, and some of them spoke of their anxiety lest the Prophet should die. The Prophet therefore went out once from his room into the mosque, supported by 'Ali and al-'Abbas. He sat on the lower step of the pulpit and Muslims gathered round him. The Prophet then reminded them of the fact that it was only Allah who was eternal, and that all other living things must die.

On the morning of Monday, thirteenth of the third month of the eleventh year of Hijrah (8 June 632 A.D.) the Prophet passed peacefully away, and the Muslim world suffered its gravest loss. The Prophet's departure was a supreme shock for all who survived him.

The Prophet died; but his memory remained fresh and supremely venerated in the minds of the millions of those who followed him throughout the generations. Muhammad died; but the impact of this modest man who was often seen mending his clothes, repairing his shoes, sweeping his house and helping his wives in domestic work, was very soon felt not only throughout the countries of the Middle East and Europe but also in China, India and in the heart of the Dark Continent, Africa. Muhammad died, leaving a perfect system of teaching which is illuminating and virtuous, progressive and practical, and which, if intelligently followed, leads to peace, prosperity and happiness. In a short span of time, this teaching transformed a great part of the world and rapidly raised mankind higher on the ladder of civilization. Knowledge and enlightenment soon became widespread. Justice and propriety widely prevailed. Much of the cruelty and evils of the ancient times was removed, and the dignity of man was largely restored.

[1] *E.g., al-Sīrah al-Nabawiyyah, pt. II, pp.* 539–97.
[2] *Shaikh Muhammad al-Khudarī, Nūr al-Yaqun, (Cairo,* 1953*), p.* 255.
[3] *Abū Dāwūd, Sunan, Vol. III, pp.* 412–3.
[4] *Encyclopaedia of Islam, s.v. Kadar;* A. Guillaume, *Some Remarks on Free Will and Predestination in Islam,* art in *J.R.A.S.,* 1924, *p.* 43.
[5] *Encyclopaedia of Religion and Ethics, s.v. Ethics and Morality.*
[6] *Chapter XXI, v.* 98.
[7] *See, e.g.,* Washington Irving, *Life of Mahomet,* London, 1850, *pp.* 94–6.
[8] *al-Sīrah al-Nabawiyyah, pt. II, p.* 603.
[9] *Matu al-Bukhārī, Vol. I, p.* 126.

# Bibliography

(a) Books

ABŪ DĀWŪD. *Sunan.* Cairo, 1950.

AMIN, AHMAD. *Fajr al-Islam.* Cairo, 1952.

BROCKELMANN, KARL. *History of the Muslim Peoples.* London, 1952.

BUKHARI, AL-, MUHAMMAD IBN ISMĀIL. *al-Saḥīh.* al-Halabi Press, Cairo, n.d., under the title: *Mutn al-Bukhārī.*

DERMENGHEM, EMILE. *The Life of Mahomet.* Routledge, London. 1930.

CUILLAUME, ALFRED. *Life of Muḥammad.* Oxford University Press, 1955.

HAIKAL, MUḤAMMAD HUSAIN. *Hayāt Muḥammad.* Cairo, 1956.

HITTI, K. PHILIP. *History of the Arabs.* Macmillan, London, 1956.

IBN HISHĀM. *al-Sīrah al-Nabawiyyah,* ed. by M. al-Saqqa in 2 pts. Cairo, 1955.

IBN KHALDUN. *Kitāb al-'Ibar wa Diwān al-Mubtada' wa al-Khabar.* Cairo, 1936.

IRVING, WASHINGTON. *Life of Mahomet.* London, 1850.

KHUDARI, AL-, SHAIKH MUḤAMMAD. *Nūr al-Yaqun fi-Sirat Sayyid al-Mursalīn.* Cairo, 1953.

LEWIS, B. *The Arabs in History.* Hutchinson, London, 1950.

MUIR, SIR WILLIAM. *Life of Mohammad.* Edinburgh, 1923.

NAWAWI, AL-, ABU ZAKARIYYA. *Riyād al Salihin.* Cairo, n.d.

NISĀBŪRĪ, AL-, ABŪ ISHĀQ, *Qisas al-Anbiyā'.* Cairo, 1951.

*Qur'ān, The.* Official Egyptian Edition, 1937 A.D.

ZUBAIRI, AL-, ABU 'ABD ALLĀH. *Kitāb Nasab Quraish.* Cairo, 1953.

(b) Encyclopaedia

*Encyclopaedia of Islam.*
*Encyclopaedia of Religion and Ethics.*

# Glossary of Arabic Terms

Adhān, (call to prayers), 57
Amīn, al-, (the trustworthy one), 23
Ansār, (Supporters, i.e., the Madinan Muslims), 49, 55, 59, 73

Ḥadīth, (Recorded sayings, practice and silent approval of the Prophet), 31
al-Hijrah, (Muhammad's emigration to Madīnah), 54

Islām, (name of Muhammad's faith), *passim*
Isrā', (the nocturnal journey to Jerusalem), 43

Jāhili, (belonging to the pre-Islamic era of ignorance), 56
Jihad, (military activities in defence of the faith), 101
Jizyah, (poll tax paid by non-Muslims in a Muslim state instead of the obligatory alms and the duty of defence), 101

Maghāzī, al-, (the Battles), 67
Majlis, (Consultative council), 7
Mi'rāj, (Muḥammad's ascent to Heaven), 43
Muhājirūn, (Emigrants, i.e., Meccan Muslims who emigrated to Madinah), 49, 55
Munāfiqūn, (the Hypocrites), 61

Nadwah, (designation of the council of the chiefs of Mecca), 14

Qiblah, (direction of the Ka'bah to be faced in formal prayers), 61

Ribā, (interest on loans), 102
Rifādah, (providing food for pilgrims), 14

Siqāyah, (providing water for the pilgrims), 14

Ummah, (the Muslim Nation), 56

# INDEX

Aaron, (Hārūn), 30
'Abbās, al-, 22, 72, 85, 104
'Abd Manāf, 15, 46
'Abd al-Muṭṭalib, 15, 17, 19, 20, 21, 22, 46
'Abd Shams, 15
'Abdullāh b. 'Abdul Muṭṭalib, (Muḥammad's father), 17, 19, 20, 21, 22, 24, 46
——b. Abu Bakr, 52
——b. Jahsh, 66, 68
——b. Muḥammad, 24
——b. Ubayy, 46, 61, 63, 76
Abraham, (Ibrāhīm), 2, 9, 10, 11, 12, 13, 20, 30
Abū al-'Aṣ b. al-Rabī, 73
Abū Bakr, 32, 33, 36, 37, 38, 43, 51, 52, 53, 72, 87, 102, 104
Abū Jahl, ('Amr b. Hishām), 35, 44, 51, 71, 73,
Abū Lahab, 34, 37
Abū Sufyān, 71, 73, 74, 78, 80, 88, 94, 95
Abū Ṭālib, 22, 23, 31, 32, 35, 40–41, 43
Abyssinia, 5, 38, 40, 41, 43, 44, 82, 84
Adam, 13, 29, 30

Africa, 105
'A'ishah, d. Abū Bakr, 43, 54, 76, 85, 87
Alī b. Abū Ṭālib, 31, 32, 33, 51, 87, 99, 104
Allāh, 12, 29, 32, 34, 37, 41, 47, 53, 62, 72, 95, 96, 101, 104
Aminah, 20, 21, 22
'Amr b. al-'Āṣ, 41, 83
'Aqabah, 47, 48, 49
Arabia, 2 ff., 12, 14, 19, 20, 31, 61, 62, 68, 82, 83, 86, 88, 96, 97, 98, 99, 100
'Arafah, 102
Asad, 23
Aws, 45, 47, 55
Badr, 71, 73, 74, 82, 85, 88, 93, 98
Bahrein, 82
Bilāl b. Rabāḥ, 57
Bu'āth, 46, 47
Busra, 82f
Byzantium, 5, 19, 61, 82, 97, 98
China, 7, 105
Christ, 2, 29, 101
Damascus, 82
David, (Dāwūd), 30
Dawmat al-Jandal, 76
Egypt, 82
Elias, (Ilias), 30

Elijah, (Iliasa'), 30
Enoch, 30
Europe, 105
Ezekiel, 30
Fāṭimah, (d. the Prophet), 24
Fāṭimah, ('Umar's sister), 39
Gabriel, (Jibril), 28, 30
Ghassanids, the, 5, 19, 45
Ghatafan, 74, 78
Ḥafṣah, 85
Hājar, 10
Ḥalīmah, 21
Ḥamzah, 85
Hāshim, 15, 19, 34, 40, 46, 51
Hawāzin, 96
Hayiyy b. Akhṭab, 78f
Hell, 29, 34, 101
Hind, 85
Hirā', Cave of, 25, 26
Hishām b. al-Walid, 73
Hūd, 30
Hudaibiyah, 78f. 93, 97, 98
Hunain, 96
Ibrāhim b. Muḥammad, 85
India, 7, 105
Irāq, 5, 45
Isaac, (Isḥāq), 10, 30
Ishmael, (Ismā'īl), 9, 10, 11, 13, 20, 30
Jacob, (Ya'qub), 30
Ja'far b. Abū Talib, 41, 84

Jeddah, 97
Jerusalem, 43, 61
Jesus, ('Isā), 30
Job, (Ayyūb), 30
John the Baptist, (Yahyā), 30
Jonah, (Yūnus), 30
Joseph, (Yūsuf), 30
Jurhum, 10, 11, 13, 14, 15
Juwairiyah, 85, 88
Ka'bah, the, 9ff., 19, 21, 40, 51, 61, 80, 81, 94, 95
Khadijah, 23f., 28, 31, 33, 43, 73, 85, 86, 87, 98
Khaibar, 84
Khalid b. al-Walid, 73
Khālid b. Zaid, (Abū Ayyūb), 53, 83, 84, 95
Khazraj, 45ff., 55
Khuza'ah, 13, 14, 93
Kindah, 45
Lakhmids, 5, 45
Lot, (Lūt), 30
Madīnah, al-, (Yathrib), 41, 54ff.
Maimūnah, 85
Maisarah, 24
Mālik, b. al-Dughunnah, 44
Ma'rib, 45
Marr al-Zahrān, 94
Marwah, al-, 10
Mecca, (Makkah), 9ff., 97ff.
Moses, (Mūsā), 30

Muḍar, 13
Muṣʿab b. ʿUmair, 48
Muṣṭaliq, 76, 87, 88
Muʾtah, 84, 96
Mutʿim b. ʿAdiyy, 44
Muṭṭalib, al-, 35, 40
Madhhij, 99
Naḍīr, al-, 45, 75, 78, 79
Najjār, 46
Najrān, 38, 44
Nakhlah, 66, 68, 71
Nawfal, 50
Negus, the, 38, 41, 82
Noah, (Nuh), 30
Oman, 82
Palestine, 45
Palmera, 5
Paradise, 29, 34
Persia, 5, 61, 82, 97, 98
Petra, 5
Qainuqāʾ, 45, 73, 74, 76
Qāsim, al-, 24
Qubāʾ, 53
Quraidhah, 45, 79, 80
Quraish, 13, 14, 15, 34, 40, 42, 49, *passim*
Qurʾan, the, 6, 31, 35, 36, 38, 39, 47, 48, 65, 69, 99, 100, 102
Quṣayy, 14, 15, 19, 51
Red Sea, the, 9, 97
Rome, 5
Ruqayyah, 24, 38
Sabaʾ, 4, 49

Saʿd, 21
Ṣafā, 10, 34
Ṣāfiyyah, 85
Ṣāliḥ, 30
Salmān, 78
Sanʿāʾ, 96
Sarah, 10
Sawdah, d. Zamʿah, 43, 53, 85
Shuʿaib, 30
Solomon, (Sulaimān), 30
Sulaim, 74
Syria, 2, 3, 9, 10, 19, 20, 22, 23, 54, 65, 76, 83, 97
Tabūk, 97, 102
Ṭāhā, 20th. Chapter in the Qurʾan, 39
Ṭāʾif, al-, 42, 43, 47, 50, 66, 96
Taim, 32
Thaqif, 42, 96
Thawr, cave of, 52
Uhud, 75, 79
ʿUmar b. al-Khaṭṭāb, 39, 54, 87
Umayyah, 15, 71
Umm Aiman, 21, 22
Umm Ḥabibah, 85, 88
Umm Kulthūm, 24
Umm Salamah, 85, 88
Usāmah b. Zaid, 62
ʿUthman b. ʿAffan, 38, 87
Walīd, al-, b. al-Walīd, 73, 81

Yamāmah, al-, 82
Yathrib, (see Madīnah), 15, 21, 22, 43, 45, 46, 47
Yemen, the, 4, 5, 9, 17, 38, 44, 45
Zachariah, (Zakariyya), 30
Zaid b. Hārithah, 31, 33, 42, 84, 88, 89
Zainab d. Jahsh, 85, 88
———d. Khuzaimah, 85, 88
———d. Muḥammad, 24, 72
Zamzam, 10, 13, 14, 15, 19
Zuhrah, 20